Mind Control Language Patterns

by Dantalion Jones

www.MindControlLanguagePatterns.com

Mind Control Language Patterns

Mind Control Publishing

Copyright   Dantalion Joness 2008

ISBN 978-0-615-24665-9

Formatted using Open Office

www.MindControlLanguagePatterns.com

Mind Control Language Patterns

First Words

After writing on persuasion and mind control in my last books (*Mind Control 101* and *The Forbidden Book of Getting What You Want*) I had considered different to go in my writing. Fiction was one possibility that is still being toyed with in the back of my twisted mind.

But the problem was there are still areas of mind control that need to be shared.

I decided to go into more depth in the area of persuasion and mind control called "Language Patterns." It's a good time to make clear what will not be in this book. First, this is a book about how to use language to influence people. There will be very little expositions on anchoring or other NLP processes. I want to focus exclusively on how to use language alone to influence people.

A good friend and linguistics professor starts his classes by saying, "The amazing thing about language and our ability to communicate isn't how well we can communicate our thoughts. It's that we can communicate using language at all." He's right. There is so much opportunity for misunderstanding and misinterpretation that it's a wonder we can talk for hours on abstract ideas and believe we understand each other.

That said, there is a great deal that can be accomplished with language when used precisely.

Amid all of language's complexity, there are processes that, when skillfully used, tend to yield very interesting and useful results. These processes, or language patterns, are what we are going to explore.

The study and application of these patterns is both a science and an art. It is a science in that much of it can be broken down into basic components and reassembled to create testable and replicable results. It is an art in that there are uncontrollable human variables that cannot always be predicted, but which can easily be managed given the experience and creativity of the user.

www.MindControlLanguagePatterns.com

Mind Control Language Patterns

Some think of persuasion through language as akin to witchcraft because the results of study and application can be so dramatic, and in many ways I agree.

Let's regress for a moment back to the pre-language world of our infancy. While in that life everything that was experienced could only be communicated through our most primal abilities: laughing and crying. As we learned language we became able to describe, and even alter, our reality by the words we use to describe it. As we grow we continue to alter our reality with words modifying it. We constantly make choices whether or not to use words like "sad," "depressed," and "suicidal," or "satisfied," "joyful," and "elated." Each of these words have a similar meaning but the reality experienced through them is quite different.

Like illusionists our words modify our reality and the reality of others, much as if they were ancient alchemical incantations. Homer's tale of the Argonauts describes *The Sirens*, whose voices can compel any man to act even against his own best interest. But that's only in mythology, right? You're invited to learn these powerfully persuasive language patterns as if they are secret incantations that will magically enchant or curse those who are to hear only your voice.

Dantalion Jones
Seattle WA
February 2008

Mind Control Language Patterns

Note To Reader

You should be warned. Although I attempt to provide as much detail as possible in the theory and application of persuasion language patterns, please understand that this is very advanced material.

If you're a beginner to this field then by all means read and learn as much as you can from it. You'll also likely benefit from supplementing your studies with the decent books on NLP and persuasion that are recommended in the back of this book. As a beginner you are encouraged to memorize the language patterns that are of greatest interest to you. By memorizing them they can become second nature, and from there you'll effortlessly begin creating your own language patterns on the fly and as you need them.

For the reader who is skilled in the theory and practice of NLP, hypnosis, influence and persuasion, and even therapists who are paid to help people change, you'll find this an adventurous ride through the forest of words that effect men's minds.

The best way to judge the language patterns you'll learn is to imagine as you read that they are being spoken to you with a passionate and sincere tone. You'll learn that if they effect you in some way then they can be even more effective when you use them to affect others.

The last point I want to make is on ethics and morality. While I encourage you to use these tools with ethics I can't enforce it. Language, like any tool, can be used to help or harm. It is essentially amoral. You'll read exactly how to both use and misuse these patterns, how to help and harm using language. Beyond that it is within your judgment (hopefully your better judgment) how you use them.

Good luck!

Mind Control Language Patterns

Dedication

To all those wonderful friends and brothers living "behind the veil" who have brought me from darkness to light and who taught me that there is no greater ambition than to cast a boulder into the current of time and alter the course of history. They have shown me the programs we live by and the programs behind the programs. They have shown me that while we all value free will very few truly have it ...or want it.

Also

To my faithful djinn, familiar and constant companion, Dantalion, the seventy-first spirit of the Goetia, "His Office is to teach all Arts and Sciences unto any; and to declare the Secret Counsel of any one; for he knoweth the Thoughts of all Men and Women, and can change them at his Will. He can cause Love, and show the Similitude of any person, and show the same by a Vision, let them be in what part of the World they Will."

Mind Control Language Patterns

Table of Contents

www.MindControlLanguagePatterns.com

Mind Control Language Patterns

Mind Control Language Patterns

Introduction

Language patterns are a unique form of covert hypnotic suggestion. You will hear them referred to by the terms "conversational hypnosis," "covert hypnosis," "Ericksonian hypnosis," "covert persuasion or influence," or my favorite, "mind control."

In traditional hypnosis the hypnotist gives direct suggestions and tells the subject what to do and how to respond. Language patterns differ because they are not direct. Instead, the operator often describes a process, and in order for the subject listening to understand what you're saying, they have to go through the process in their mind, and end up convincing themselves.

The popularity of covert language patterns evolved from NLP practitioners using them for seduction. They were packaged into "get laid" NLP products and seminars designed for the horny male too busy to take an NLP course and figure it out for themselves.

Likely you have heard the claim that only seven percent of a message's meaning is received from the verbal content, thirty-eight percent from vocal cues, and fifty-five percent from facial expressions.

This book openly disputes that claim.

Voltaire said, "Give me ten minutes to talk away my ugly face, and I will bed the Queen of France." While other factors can influence the results of your communication, it is the spoken word that gets results. Also, keep in mind that Voltaire did say he would have to talk to the Queen, meaning he would have to be in front of her to make his presentation. This is important, because there is a mind set that is vital to the effective use of "mind control."

For those new to NLP-type persuasion there is often a belief that all one has to do is say a few language patterns and people will bend to one's will. Some newbies hope they can "get into someone's mind and drive it around."

STOP!!

Mind Control Language Patterns

If you held that belief, then understand that language patterns are entirely interactive and require both party's participation.

Consider a child's game where someone hides an object and the only clues given are "warmer," when the seeker gets close and "colder," when they move away from the object. The effectiveness of language patterns works much the same way. The user must pay attention to the other's responses. From that information, they know whether they are getting "warmer" or "colder." The difference is in the degree of subtle changes that you will be observing. For many, those subtle changes have never been given proper attention, but the truth is that this information makes all the difference in getting what you want.

Your ability to notice how someone is reacting is essential to your effectiveness. When you begin to see the subtle flush of the cheek, for example, it's a sign that something is happening. You may not know immediately what the person is feeling - it could be anger, embarrassment, arousal, or simply a hot flash. It could be good or bad. All you know is that something is happening! To ignore it, as most do, would be a fatal flaw in getting what you want. It would be equally wrong to read too much into it. Don't fall prey to "mind reading," where you make assumptions about what people think. It could be completely untrue. In the late 1960s came a barrage of books on body language that proclaimed that someone sitting with crossed arms and legs is closed to learning. These were the best books at the time, but many people have proved these simplistic statements wrong. Anyone can sit with their arms and legs crossed and still learn. Try it for yourself.

Language patterns work for many reasons, a primary one being that **they bring about an emotional state and then suggest an action to accompany the emotion.** The truth is that someone can be talked into bed, a business partnership, or sold a product or service - just with words.

If one controls the emotions of others, then they are very likely to follow suggestions. This is because people almost universally make their decisions based on feelings, rather than reason. The skillful manipulation of emotions can drive a nation to war or to build giant monuments and institutions. Individuals in one-on-one encounters are no different, and gaining control is then often easier, because feedback is instant.

Mind Control Language Patterns

Most people learn language patterns by first memorizing existing patterns and, if they're smart, practicing them. After some practice, one quickly understands the theory behind the patterns and begins to generate creative patterns on their own.

Dark and Light Language Patterns

When NLP was discovered, a few people began to play with the techniques and patterns in ways that were "less than helpful."

In fact, they devised and applied these skills in completely harmful and wicked ways, like finding ways to create phobias of poverty for those people who want to be rich. Worse, they would create phobias in people with no positive intent. This brought about the field of "Dark NLP," also known as "Black Ops Patterns".

There are several reason that this book is going to discuss and reveal "Black Ops Patterns." Yes, you *could* use them on others but it's just better to know when they are being done on you. Suffice to say that if you use these patterns on people it can be the end of the line for any further productive relationship. Take note.

Mind Control Language Patterns

The Foundational Mindset

If there were only one section of this book that you could read in order to get the best benefit, then this is it, and it has nothing to do with language patterns! It is about your mindset, the mental attitude and beliefs you take on that allow language patterns to work their magic and make yourself incredibly effective.

Language patterns are merely the outer game of mind control and persuasion. It is in your inner game that lies the difference that makes the difference.

You're about to discover a list of beliefs that make the difference between being effective with language patterns, or merely reciting words. Sit back. Read them. Recite them. Let them echo in your own mind and become your own beliefs. You can choose to believe them by simply believing them. It's that easy.

1. You will create for anyone the best, most profound and real experience they will have in their life.
2. No other person can give the kind of experience you can.
3. You can do this.
4. You know it works beyond any doubt, question or hesitation.
5. Others will believe that you and your abilities are amazing.
6. It is normal for you to give anyone exactly the type of experience you want them to have.
7. Given the place, time and situation, you can do this with anyone, without hesitation or doubt.

Something else that further empowers your words is your intention. In NLP terms this is referred to as "having a clearly formed outcome." More specifically, it means knowing what you want the other person to do and holding that in your mind.

It also means having your outcome express itself as an assumption that is subtly expressed in your emotions and actions. For example, let's assume you want a romantic encounter. If you hold in your mind this intention as you talk, then your actions will begin to be colored by that intent. Because this process is interactive, the intent will affect both

Mind Control Language Patterns

you and them. Part of your intent is to pull your subject, through actions, into a shared reality that you have created.

Using Language Patterns

As you go through these language patterns, you'll want to go out and use them just for the sake of using them, and you can. What you'll find is that you can only measure your effectiveness if you have an outcome in mind. You can start with simple outcomes, if you like. Like getting a smile. From there, feel free to explore, but always keep your outcome in mind

.

Fear of Using Language Patterns

Many hesitate to use language patterns, because they're afraid of getting caught or because it feels different from how they normally communicate. My advise on these two points is, first, you won't get caught and second, get over it!

Anything worth learning is worth doing poorly. Consider for a moment the benefits you'll receive in being able to effectively communicate in order to get what you want. Yes, there are many. Among them...

- The ability to get what you want.
- The ability to feel comfortable with anyone as you communicate with them.
- The ability to see subtle changes in their behavior that help guide you to influence them.
- The ability to change peoples' minds.
- The ability, if cornered, to make someone feel depressed and confused.

Go back and then re-read the seven beliefs mentioned above.

Mind Control Language Patterns

More on The Mind Set of Persuasive Language Patterns.

Have you ever been in conversation with someone who made you feel as if you were the most important person in the world and that they were speaking to the deepest parts of your soul? Being able to create this feeling in others makes delivering language patterns easier and more forceful.

The endless debate on how to do it all boils down to one word: *charisma.* To understand this powerful quality, consider how most people communicate. Often their attention is on two levels. On one level, they are directly communicating their thoughts, insights and information to the other person. On another level, they are indirectly communicating all the other things that are on their minds. Perhaps they had a fight with a spouse that day or are worried about bills. These semi-conscious thoughts act to distract and prevent them from fully focusing on the other person. For you reading this book - focus fully on the other person.

When you put aside all distractions, by sheer force of will, if necessary, your awareness opens to more subtle cues from the individual, and your ability to influence them is multiplied.

Combine this sense of focus with your own unstoppable conviction, and your words take on a power of their own.

The first step is to recognize that these distractions exist. The next step is to vow that, while you are attempting to influence someone, you put your distractions aside in order to focus only on them and how to direct them toward your outcome. See to it that nothing deters your focus.

By the way, when practicing, it's important to remember that your purpose is to pay attention and not to stare them down.

Many teachers of persuasion will tell you that sincerity is a vital component of effective persuasion. Yes, sincerity is important even when you don't believe what you are saying! Con-men have the ability to believe what they are saying, sincerely, even if they only believe it for that moment.

Know that it's much easier to be sincere, when you actually are sincere, but it's not essential.

Mind Control Language Patterns

The Dual Reality Principle

What you say is always subject to interpretation, and the interpretation is completely dependent upon the perspective of the listener. When more than one person hears you, there can be many different interpretations, and this can be used to your advantage. Nothing demonstrates this concept more than what stage magicians call "The Dual Reality Principle."

The Dual Reality Principle is when two people have heard one thing, yet by design they each come to different conclusions.

One can notice this when language patterns are being used. For example, a man is using language patterns to win a date. A bystander hearing the conversation may think the guy is a little strange, talking about things that are typically non-guy topics, like "connection," "passion" and "the warmth of feelings." However, the woman likely has a completely different perception of the conversation.

Stage magicians make use of this effect all the time, when they allow the audience to perceive something "magical," while the volunteer on stage perceives that they are merely following orders.

An example of this would be when, without giving away an entire magic trick, the magician asks a volunteer to reach into the magician's pocket to prove to the audience that it's empty. As the volunteer does so, the magician says, "Don't do anything, okay!" This, of course, gets a laugh from the audience, as they envision the volunteer's hands potentially injuring the magicians nether regions. He then tells the volunteer, "Okay, take your hand out," and then he proclaims to the audience, "Your hand is empty."

What the audience doesn't know is that the pocket wasn't empty but had a deck of cards in it. The volunteer could even feel the deck of cards, but when he heard the magician tell him, "Don't do anything, okay?" he heard it to mean, "just put your hand in my pocket...nothing else." When the magician tells the volunteer, "your hand is empty" the volunteer thinks nothing of it but the audience hears it to mean, "there is nothing in my pocket."

Understanding the Dual Reality Principle will give you a higher level of thinking about communication and language patterns. Implementing this principle may take some time and planning, but is always fun. To use it, you must take on three perspectives: your perspective and what you will say; the second person's perspective and how you want them to perceive what you are saying; and the third person's perspective and how you want them to perceive what you say.

Mind Control Language Patterns

Taking Mind Control From the Laboratory to The Streets
Mind Control Theory

Mind control theory is simple and can be described as having four basic levels of perception and influence. First, consider the basic theory behind mind control, which is very simple, and then we'll dive into about the practice of it, which the remainder of this book is dedicated to describing.

The first level of perception and influence is the most superficial; this is where stimulus meets the senses. This is quite simple and straightforward in theory - people respond to what their senses perceive. On a practical level of influence and mind control this means limiting what the subject perceives with the five senses, so that they can make conclusions and assumptions based only on that information. This is what many cults attempt to do and many of the paranoid conspiracy theorists believe the so-called Illuminati are doing to everybody.

The second level is an attempt to define the meaning of the sensory perceptions. In other words, if you introduce someone to people jumping up and down with drums beating, then you can define it as dancing or demon possession, and the definition will be accepted, as long as the subject has no prior reference to the stimuli. If the subject does have some prior associations, then they are likely to bring that information into the meaning they create.

This third level is one in which the subject develops their own meaning and interpretation of the information. This personal interpretation may incorporate level two definitions. Here the individual compares the sensory information and it's given meaning to their own preexisting beliefs, perceptions and experiences, in order to draw a conclusion. For example, a beating with a cane may include pain (first level perception) and be prescribed as a punishment (second level perception), but the subject may associate it with an experience in their youth, where they were whipped by an attractive nanny and experienced arousal. Thus, their third level perception would be one of arousal, instead of punishment.

At the fourth level of perception, strong emotions and beliefs are associated with the external stimuli and thus ingraining them deeper in the individual psyche. At this level, these beliefs and emotions become like elected politicians, who spend a great deal of energy trying to maintain their power. It is at this level that habits, obsessions and phobias take hold.

Mind Control Practice

When bringing the above theory into practice, it is always wise to consider the design of every part of what the subject will experience with their senses. This is why a salesman in his own sales office will sell more than visiting prospects. In a sales office (or church, temple, recruiting center, bed room, etc.) the subject has no control over the environment and must often yield to the experience that the sales office creates for them.

At this level, influence has less to do with language and language patterns than what the total five senses are perceiving. At this level one can create the "pacing and dragging" experience for the subject. Pacing and dragging (which is not exactly pacing and leading) occurs when the subject figuratively agrees to step into the door (pacing) and then is brought from one experience to another with such force, speed and intensity (dragging) that they must agree to the conclusions of what they experience. This is how some criminals create a compelling reality, which makes their mark feel safe enough to give up his money.

At the second level, language patterns can be applied. The most simple application of language patterning is done by calling an experience or perception good, bad, holy, demonic, important, worthless, or something else. Practical application at this level of influence is often done long before the actual experience. For example, many young women are raised to anticipate their wedding as a sacred, special and important event, and as a result, they minimize the work, trouble and expenses that anyone else would consider a pain in the ass. As a lesson to the mind controller, it's important to set up this level of influence as early as possible, so the subject is ready to experience it as you prescribe.

The third level of influence can be the most challenging to control, because it is difficult to know how the subject will incorporate the information they receive. While you can prescribe a meaning to the experience, it does not guarantee that it will be accepted or that variations in the meaning will not be made. As a practical matter, getting feedback is very important. The meaning the experience is given can be nudged in one direction or the other with accurate information. If the subject has a strong preexisting opposition to that direction, then change can be very difficult.

Assuming the subject's personal meaning of the events doesn't oppose how you want to persuade them, the fourth level of influence can be the most powerful and enduring. For that reason, it can also be the most perilous. To succeed can mean a long lasting and beneficial alliance. To fail could create an enemy that obsessively wants to hurt you. At this level you can ingrain beliefs and emotions into the subject that make the resulting behaviors self sustaining.

The Ideal Persuasion

We can describe what could be the ideal model of persuasion, using these four levels of perception and influence.

Level One

Every aspect of what the subject will perceive is engineered to lead to the most desirable result. Think of this as arranging the ideal date. But it also applies to sales, cult indoctrination, political campaigning, and police interrogation.

Level Two

You give your meaning to the events, describe it in all the glorious or gruesome terms that would best suit your needs. If possible, you inoculate your subject by describing their experience and how they will interpret it, before they have it. Useful language patterns include presuppositions, values elicitation, and elicitation of the feeling of anticipation.

Level Three

Here, the subject begins to make associations to the experience, based on their previous experience. Language patterns can be used to guide the subject's associations, based on your prior knowledge of their history.

Level Four

The subject assigns beliefs and meanings for the experience you created for them. With those meanings, they also have the emotional experience you wanted. The experience and its meaning become solid for them, as something that is important. Emotional elicitation and anchoring would be a few of the language patterns useful on this level.

Mind Control Language Patterns

Providing and Deleting Options

So now you're aware of four levels of perception and four levels of influence that can be used to give you more power and control. A sense of power comes about when you become aware of what other people don't usually consider. Because most people aren't aware of these levels of perception, your power can grow by increasing or decreasing the options that you offer people at these levels. What follows are four types of information. With each level, the information gets more complex.

Binary Information (All or Nothing, Good or Bad, Black or White)

This is the most limiting of information options. It means the information will only fall into one category, or it will not. Used in its darkest form, a religious cult will ask its members to divide everything into us/them categories. In terms of language patterns, it means describing something in binary terms - good or bad.

Better/Worse Information

There is more flexibility when there are more options. Here, choices are not binary but have a rank - this one is better than that one. What is absent with this information is how much better/worse something is, compared to its counterpart. There is no gradient or scale.

Scaled Information (rating on 1 to 100)

Here, the information is provided on a gradient scale that starts at zero, or nothing, and goes to any extreme. With this quality of information you can provide information that is "good enough" or "not bad enough," and thus influence a decision the subject can make.

Complex Relationship Information

This is the level of information with the greatest degree of variability and therefore, the greatest freedom and flexibility. This quality of

Mind Control Language Patterns

information contains certain traits that can be ranked on a gradient, and there are relationships between certain traits.

Using this model of mind control and the various levels of perception, you can add and delete information with varied qualities at the various levels of information. Thus if someone is stuck at seeing something in binary terms (good or bad), you can go up enough levels to give them flexibility of choice. Once they are directed to the decision you want, you can go back down to the binary level of information and call it "good."

It should be noted, the difference between counseling/therapy and mind control. Generally, therapy is designed to help a person move from a narrower to a broader range of perspectives, all for the benefit of the individual. Mind Control, by comparison, is interested in the results as it relates to the controller, and perspectives can be broadened and narrowed to suit the end result. To better understand this process, let's look at some example.

> *(Binary Information) There is an experience that almost everyone has shared of overhearing an interesting conversation and knowing what every word means, but still having to focus in on the words, so that you can follow what is being said. (Better/Worse Information). You then realize that you've moved from hearing just the words to understanding the concepts and principles that are being discussed. And so the topic becomes interesting to you. (Scaled Information), so as you pay more attention, you start to learn. The words which were really just sounds now have even greater meaning, because this is something new to you that's interesting. (Complex Information). Now you can begin to wonder how it is you are able to take in information so well, and use it to make changes in your life. That type of information has a quality all it's own.*

Here is an example taken from the book "Understanding Advanced Hypnotic Language Patterns" by John Burton Ed.D.

> *(Binary Information) Have you ever been riding in a car... , but you were a passenger in the car, maybe in the front seat ... and you were just looking out the window,*

down at the roadside, watching the edge of the road as you passed along? You noticed how incredibly fast the road passed beneath you, how landmark after landmark flew by. It seemed extremely fast. (Better/Worse Information). Then maybe you decided to look just a bit further off the road - maybe to a front yard, as you passed by. And then the next front yard, as you passed, noticing that the yards passed by more slowly. It took longer for them to go by - or really, for you to go by them. (Scaled Information). And then maybe you decided to look even further off the roadside and noticed the houses, or beyond these, behind the houses. And you noticed how much more slowly these passed, or you actually passed them. This seems much slower (Complex Information), and then you decided to look even further off in the distance, perhaps to the uttermost edge of the horizon or maybe up at a cloud in the sky, way off in the distance. You know how clouds can sometimes appear in the shapes of something else familiar, like a dog or a boat or something else? And you can start at a cloud way off in the distance, not really knowing quite what shape it is taking, but also noticing that it seems to be completely still, not moving at all, and how paradoxical this stillness feels. You know you are moving, and yet at the same time, completely still - completely still, as you fix your eyes upon this cloud that remains in constant view, knowing that there are other clouds in other places that are in constant view as well, appearing completely still. And now a soft, still, calm feeling steals down inside, and you find you may absorb this feeling, just like a soft, absorbent cloud within you that soaks up the feeling, saturating your very being with this comforting, floating, calm, deeply relaxing sensation. As you let go, you realize this is everywhere.

Mind Control Language Patterns

Using Your Voice To Control Emotions: Tones and Pacing

While the focus will be on the words themselves, you'll find that the tonality and pace of speech are very important when delivering language patterns. Please note that what is described here is specifically for English. Other languages have their own rules regarding voice tonality.

The Flat Tone

Consider the words, "You will lift that bag." If spoken in a flat monotone, then it simply describes what will happen, as if reading from a to-do list.

The Rising Tone

It begins to sound like a question, when you say, "You will lift that bag," with a rising tone. This could be a question or a statement, said in a rising tone. A question is an acknowledgment of uncertainty, so even if spoken like a statement, it sounds uncertain and weak..

The Downward Tone

When spoken with a downward tone, "You will lift that bag" becomes an order, command or imperative.

An understanding of rising, downward and flat tones will give you a clue about how to modify the impact of the words you use. Perhaps you want to make a suggestion but don't want to give it a strong impact. In that case, you say it in a rising (questioning) tone. For example, saying "Maybe you can choose this path?" has a different impact than when said in lowering tones.

Pace of Speech

The pace of speech has a stronger impact than one might think. One way of noticing this is by speaking at the pace of your breathing. Begin by simply noticing your breath when not speaking. The length of the inhale will be as long as the exhale. When speaking, we modify our breathing, because we only speak when exhaling. Therefore, inhales will be shorter than the exhales. When we pace our voice to the natural rhythm of our breathing, the attention of the listener is subtly altered.

Mind Control Language Patterns

When speaking, there is a pause during the inhale, which is usually not noticed, but tends to have the unconscious effect of creating anticipation. When it is followed by speech or the continuation of the sentence, there is an unconscious sense of relief.

As you speak at the pace of your breath, you are creating a subtle cycle of anticipation and relief in the listener. They are anticipating your next words and feeling relief when they hear it.

That is quite a compelling power. When it is working, you will most likely notice the face of the listener, gazing intently and hanging on to your every word, without blinking.

Another example of pace of speech is often referred to as "the voice roll," that is very common among evangelical preachers. The pace of the voice roll is a bit faster than the pace of breath, but the effect is the same. Voice roll is usually delivered at the rate of forty-five to sixty beats per minute, in order to maximize the hypnotic effect.

EXERCISE:

Listen to your own voice as you speak. Most people have a very monotone voice, even when they are passionate about what they are speaking. Pick a sentence to read aloud and change the tonality of each word. Read it with a questioning tone. Then read it as if it were a command. Begin to notice how the tonality of your voice can impact the meaning of what you are saying.

Mind Control Language Patterns

The Parts Pattern - Creating Another Personality

This first pattern should be easy, because it requires only to understand a concept. You don't have to memorize anything word for word (but you can if you want).

To understand The Parts Pattern, consider that we all have "parts" within us. There is a part that finds learning patterns interesting, even fascinating. You can recognize it as the part that made you buy this book. With this part now awakened, you can notice a growing interest to learn. As you learn more patterns and how to use them, this part comes alive and grows stronger and stronger, until it becomes so overpowering, you have to go out and see how they affect people.

Now, I just made that last part up - but it's very likely that you noticed it had an effect.

The secret of "parts" creation is to realize that, when you name something, it becomes real. When you start to describe it, it comes alive. It is sort of like that childlike part of you that is curious to learn more. Before you read that last sentence, there was no "part" there, and after it was described, your mind began to connect the dots, so that the "curious childlike" part began to come into awareness.

Step one - name a part.

Step two - describe it.

The part could be the part that becomes fascinated, or the part that ignores the unimportant, or the part that becomes remorseful or depressed (if part of a "dark" pattern). Let's now make these examples come alive:

Interesting things happen when you notice something that you recognize as interesting. It's like there is a part of you that becomes fascinated, and it locks into whatever you're focusing on. When it comes alive, it's almost like you close off all your awareness of the surrounding world, and it's just this one subject that commands all your attention, and you can't ignore it. In fact, as much as you try to turn away, it just draws you closer.

Mind Control Language Patterns

When you have a clear idea about what's important, and you focus on it, there is another part of you that begins to take everything that doesn't matter and pushes it away. Have you ever noticed how, as soon as your attention becomes aware of a trivial distraction, it shrinks it in your mind and screams, "FOCUS!" and snap - you're right back on what really does matter? All you have to do is realize that what you're doing is important, and this part gets ready. This part that ignores the unimportant will take what really matters and make it grow bigger and brighter in your mind, so that nothing will distract you - and the more you try to turn away, the more important these things become.

There is a part inside your mind that knows when you've done something wrong. It's the part that feels guilt and quickly tries in vain to push it away, but only makes it more glaring, noisy and sharp in your mind. Again and again, it comes back, even when you sleep, and the more you try to suppress it, the stronger it becomes. Finally, it becomes so strong that you do everything in your power to avoid sleep, because of the guilt that grows stronger, like a cancer weighing you down. Even in those moments, when your mind is free of the guilt, this part of you is plotting to remind you of what you did. You'll never outrun it. You'll never even outlive it.

If there is one part that does something, then there can be others that have other functions. One part could activate another part, and all you have to do is describe how they interact with each other. Here is an example with a part that feels depression and a part that takes action.

Sometimes there is part of each of us that makes us feel down. For some people, it only pulls them down further and further, and a lot of people get stuck there. But there is another part inside that pulls you into action and straightens your spine and paints a clear path, focuses on simple and doable tasks. It's the first part that calls the other into action and keeps you going, no matter what.

Mind Control Language Patterns

One can darkly create two parts that loop back on each other. The first is the part that gets confused. The second is the part that feels fear and terror. One causes the other, creating a loop in which the person either feels confusion or terror. The only option is to leave the thought. The only use of this is to create amnesia to a specific thought. When the thought comes up, the confused part comes alive. The confused part then awakens the fearful, terrorized part. They cycle back and forth, creating discomfort, no matter what, until the subject stops trying to think about the suggested topic. This is a sure prescription for neurosis.

Mind Control Language Patterns

Give Them Exactly What YOU Want:
Presuppositions

To presuppose something simply means that what you want is going to happen, and you demonstrate that belief in your words and actions. This is the linguistic equivalent of an assumption. In other words, presuppositions are not directly stated but assumed within the language. For example, by using the following words, one can presuppose that something will happen or has happened: *automatically, continuously, spontaneously, steadily, instinctively, almost magically, constantly, even without thinking, second nature, unconsciously, involuntarily.*

> *Before you automatically open the refrigerator door, you should hold your nose.*

This presupposes that the refrigerator door will be opened without resistance and that something smells bad inside.

As an exercise, write three sentences that presuppose that something you want is happening automatically. Likewise, by using the following words, one can presuppose something is true, factual and proven: *actual, actually, absolute, genuine, self-evident, unimpeachable, real, really, true, truly, obviously, fact, factual, certified, proven, authentic, valid, verified, unquestionable, undeniable, definite, irrefutable.*

Thus the following sentences presuppose something about this book and the person reading it...*you.*

> *By studying this material, you'll steadily appreciate the absolute depth of the author's insights.*

Here, the presupposition of "steadily appreciate" emphasizes that you will be appreciative, and it is not questioned, because it will happen *steadily.*

Mind Control Language Patterns

The irrefutable commitment to learn is the self-evident key mark of the people who read this material.

Here, the commitment is presupposed, because it is described as *irrefutable.*

Presuppositions of Permanence

There are many benefits to presupposing permanence. If you want a long term customer, enduring satisfaction, or for someone to feel a long lasting feeling then presupposing these indestructible qualities has value.

You can suggest moving towards permanence. In other words convey how the results and the help you'll give your customers and clients will be permanent or long lasting. You can also suggest moving away from permanence. This is where you suggest that the pain they're in will persist, and will be permanent unless they let you help them. Suggesting all the permanent problems they'll get by dealing with your competitors is also a lot of fun.

As a dark application you can suggest that all their guilt, shame and fatigue be lasting and permanent.

Here are some useful words for presupposing permanence: *lasting, remaining, stable, secure, staying, indestructible, endless, nonstop, stay with, year after year, day after day, long term, continuing, eternal, ceaseless, constant, enduring, persistent.*

Note, for everything that you can presuppose don't forget that you can also imply it and simply say it straight out as well. A presupposition might be, "do you know any other provider with such a dedication to long lasting customer service?" An implication might be, "our commitment to customer service began 50 years ago when the company started, and it's part of our mission to continue to improve in that area." A direct statement might look like this, "we have a commitment to customer service for as long as you have our products."

As powerful as presuppositions are it's important to note that linguistic presuppositions alone will not get anyone laid. Presupposition patterns like "as you continue to focus your attention on me banging you..." just don't pull much weight. This is where you should make some further distinctions.

Mind Control Language Patterns

First, if you're using language to bring someone to arousal and have sex with them the linguistic presuppositions should be on the ease of feeling certain emotions and feelings in the body, and not the act of sex. For example, "It's amazing how just by thinking about it a person can begin to naturally feel an ongoing sense of comfort. Have you had a chance to notice how quickly that feeling of connectedness follows a persistent sense of ease when you're talking to someone?"

In the area of seduction there are some mental beliefs that you should presuppose that will help you. These are the Foundational Beliefs mentioned earlier. Just another good reason to go back, read them and make them a part of your personality.

SOME WORDS YOU CAN USE:

lasting, remaining, stable, secure, staying, indestructible, endless, non-stop, stay with, year after year, day after day, long term, continuing, eternal, ceaseless, constant, enduring, persistent, etc.

Notes on presuppositions:

For everything that you can presuppose, don't forget that you can also **imply** it, and simply **say it straight out**, as well.

Presuppose

Do you know any other provider with such a dedication to long lasting customer service?

Imply

Our commitment to customer service began 50 years ago when the company started, and it's part of our mission to continue to improve in that area.

Saying it Straight Out

We have a commitment to customer service for as long as you have our products.

Mind Control Language Patterns

Taking People on a Time Travel Adventure:
Verb Tenses of Past, Present and Future

Using verb tenses to change people's minds is both very advanced and very simple, because when you "get it" you can make dramatic changes in people with seemingly little effort. A good example of this is the perceptive cop who can tell a husband murdered his wife, because upon investigation at the murder scene, he says, "I loved my wife," instead of saying it in the present tense, "I love my wife."

As we speak, we are unconsciously using the verbs we've learned. These verbs have a verb tense that indicates if the action of the verb is in the past, present or future. Okay, so much for the review of grade school English. How can we apply this for persuasion?

The easiest application is in therapeutic settings where problems can be switched from being in the present to somewhere in the past, and solutions and resources can be moved into the present and available in the future.

To get a grasp on how to use verb tenses, let's think of how we perceive time. For most of us we are familiar with a "time line" with "the past" in one direction and "the future" in the other direction and "now" being where you are standing on the time line.

So someone is talking to you, and you want them to do something, but they have an objection, or if you're in a therapeutic setting, the person is talking about a problem that they have. If the problem is present, they will be talking about it in the present tense.

Mind Control Language Patterns

Notice how the experience of the problem/objection changes as the verb tense changes.

> *I procrastinate.* (**Present Tense**)
> *I procrastinated.* (**Past Tense**)
> *I will procrastinate.* (**Future Tense**).

Now notice how your experience changes when the present participle form (-ing) is added.

> *I am procrastinating.*
> *I was procrastinating.*
> *I'll be procrastinating.*

For many people, adding the -ing makes the procrastination more real and "present," regardless of when it will happen.

The procrastination can be made to feel more distant by using the past perfect:

> *I had procrastinated.* (**Past Perfect**)

This makes the action feel as if it is not only in the past but completed and, perhaps, not likely to be repeated.

> *I had had procrastinated.* (While this may not seem completely grammatical, the effect is significant).

> *I have procrastinated.* (**Present Perfect**)

Present perfect indicates that now the procrastination has ended.

> *I will have procrastinated.* (**Future Perfect**)

The future perfect indicates that at a time in the future the procrastination will reach a point when it ends.

So, using this knowledge, one could take a problem that someone states in the present tense, and begin to talk about it in the past perfect tense, as if it were over and done with. Then they could imagine a response or reaction that works better, and talk about it in the present and the future.

> Person A: I notice that every time I want to talk to a girl, I get nervous.
> Person B: So, you have had a habit of getting nervous, right?
> Person A: Yeah.
> Person B: What would you rather be feeling now, instead?
> Person A: Confidence, I guess. Yeah - excited confidence.
> Person B: Hmmm...okay, so you know what excited confidence would feel like?
> Person A: Yeah - I think so.
> Person B: So you probably can remember a situation where excited confidence was present?
> Person A: Yeah, when I was competing in debate in high school. I was very good.
> Person B: Can you remember that feeling now?
> Person A: Oh yeah!
> Person B: When you're feeling that feeling now, how do you notice it in your body and how you move?
> Person A: My mind is quieter. I stand taller. I feel like...I'm in control.
> Person B: You do, don't you?
> Person A: Yeah!
> Person B: Now, what would it be like at that time in the future, now, when you see a girl you want to talk to, and you feel this excited confidence pull you into action? It feels good, doesn't it?

This is a hypothetical conversation, and not all changes can be done so quickly. After all, mind control and persuasion is an art, not a science.

In a conversation with a friend, ask, *"What is a limitation you would like to overcome?"* and begin to speak of it only in the past tense and past perfect tense. More importantly, assume it is in the past and over with.

Next ask, *"What resource would you rather have, instead of that limitation?"* With their response, begin to revivify the resource,

Mind Control Language Patterns

asking them to remember (now) what it feels like, and describe it. Then follow by speaking about the resource as if they have it now, in the present tense, and will have it in the future. You can covertly test how well you've done at the conclusion by simply asking, *"Do you think you know what to do now?"* If they answer *"Yes,"* then you've done your job. To anyone listening, it may seem like nothing more than a simple conversation, but the effect is a dramatically therapeutic one.

Another exercise in covert use of time tenses is to first determine your outcome for the other person, and then what emotions and responses within them would facilitate that outcome.

Step 1. Elicit the emotional state.

"Do you remember a time when you felt...?"

Step 2. Bring it from the past to the present.

"What does that feel like?" and *"that's a neat feeling, isn't it?"* (Put it in the present.)

Step 3. Use the verb tense to program that feeling into the future, or link it now to your outcome.

"What would it be like at that time right now when you have a chance to decide on a widget that you see, and you feel that emotion right now? That has got to be a solid feeling, isn't it?"

Using verb tense can also be used to create problems, worries and doubt in others. All you have to do is take the good feelings and state them in the past tense, and state negative feelings in the present and future tense. In this black ops example, the feelings of insecurity are reinforced.

Person A: I'm noticing I'm feeling more confident with myself when I talk to people.
Person B: Oh you had, hadn't you?
Person A: Well, yeah.

Mind Control Language Patterns

Person B: I remember you've been feeling uncertainty when you're around people. Do you ever find yourself remembering how heavy that feels?
Person A: No, not so much.
Person B: While you're feeling that doubt and insecurity right now, how do you know you will have never gotten rid of it?
Person A: You're an asshole.

When using this, and many dark patterns, you'll find that they will quickly alienate you, but they can still accomplish your goal of creating doubt and insecurity.

As a final note on verb tenses - this is so powerful that it can accidentally be used to create problems. In fact, people do this unconsciously all the time by simply reminding others, *"What about your fear of large crowds?"* or *"Do you still have that problem?"* Of course they mean well, but the effect is to make the problem real and present.

A very simple and formulaic way to do this process for therapeutic reasons is to first ask, *"What is a challenge you're facing?"* and make sure the challenge is an internal state and potentially under their control. Then ask, *"What state or emotion would you rather have, instead?"*

These two questions will give you the challenge and the resource.

To remove the challenge, ask three questions that presuppose the challenge is in the past. *"So, you had had that challenge, right?"* *"And you remember having felt that challenge?"* *"Having remembered having felt that challenge in the past you then knew what it had felt like, right?'*

To put the resourceful response in the present, ask three questions that presuppose having and feeling the resource right now. *"Because you're mentioning this resource you know what this resource feels like and it feels pretty good, doesn't it?"* *"And as you're feeling this resource now it feels better, doesn't it?"* *"Having this resource now present can really make a difference, agreed?"*

The final step is a sentence attributed to Richard Bandler that will lock it into place in the future, *"What would it be like at that time*

Mind Control Language Patterns

in the future, right now, when you remember having had that challenge - but now you feel that resource with you at every moment... that's got to feel pretty good, doesn't it?"

After doing this process, the most interesting response I've found is that, when I ask, *"So is there really a problem?"* they say, *"No, theres no problem."* - and they truly mean it!

Black Ops Variation

Using verb tense can be done to hurt or create problems, worries and doubt in others. All you have to do is take the good feelings and state them in the past tense and negative feelings in the present and future tense.

When using this, and many dark patterns, you'll find that they will quickly alienate you, but they can still accomplish your goal of creating doubt and insecurity.

Time Distortion Variations

By playing with tenses and with how people perceive time, you can put them into a hypnotic state where there is no "now."

Think of time distortion as taking someone on a temporal roller coaster that goes from past to future to present in a seemingly chaotic order. A good example of this effect is the connection pattern that is introduced in the seduction community. The connection pattern is designed to create an emotional connection that seems as though it has been there forever. This eternal connection is created by riding the roller coaster of time distortion.

> *Have you ever noticed what it's like when you really connect with someone? It's as if there is this cord of light that connects the two of you and that cord glows warm with the feeling of this connection. You can even imagine yourself, six months from now, still feeling this connection and you can remember back to this day, right now and remember when you first felt it.*

Mind Control Language Patterns

The last sentence of this pattern is filled with ups and downs on the temporal roller coaster - first feeling the connection now, then six months from now and from there, remembering back to now, all the while feeling the connection.

The lesson you can learn from this is that, if you want to have someone feel *any* emotion or response as enduring and permanent, use time distortion.

Mind Control Language Patterns

Weaseling Into Peoples Minds:
Ericksonian Hypnotic Phrasing Examples
(a.k.a. Weasel Phrases)

What follows is a collection of language patterns used by Dr. Milton Erickson. With each of these examples, a person can make suggestions without giving a commanding order. Consider the command, *"Consider why you want to do this."* If said as a direct command, it would create a great deal of resistance - but you could say, *"I'm not entirely sure how well you can consider why you want to do this,"* or *"A friend once never told me - you want to do this!"* -thus working the command into a sentence, which does not offer the listener a chance to reject it. This explains why these are called "weasel phrases."

Complete each one of these phrases with a command:

A friend once NEVER told me to...
After you come to...
After you've...
And the more you (X) the more you (Y)
As you...
...by just noticing.
...in a way that meets your needs.
...what would have to happen to convince your Wondrous Mind
to   continue this ..."
A whole new way of thinking just opened up...
All that really matters...
All that's really important...
Allowing yourself to just naturally..
Almost as if/as though/like...
And (Name), you know better that anyone that....
And as that occurs, you really can't help but notice...
And creating change like this...
And do you notice the beginning of ...?
And I think you're going to enjoy being surprised that ....
And I want you to notice something that's happening to you.
And I wonder if you'll be curious, as you notice...
And I wonder if you'll be curious about the fact that you...

Mind Control Language Patterns

And I'd like to have you discover...
And if you wish...
And it appears that already...
And it's very rewarding to know that...
And like magic...
And maybe you'll enjoy noticing...
And so it has been done...
And sooner or later, I don't know just when....
And that growing realization
And that will probably remind you of other experiences, and other feelings you've had.
And that's just fine/all right/okay...
And the awareness that you've gained today...
And the genuine desire to really CHANGE once and for all...
And the ways in which you'll surprisingly be using these learnings...
And then, now you'll discover...
And while you continue...
And while you wonder that, I want you to discover that...
And would you be willing to experience...?
And you begin to wonder when...
And you can be pleased ....
And you can really use it...
And you can wonder what...
And you can wonder....
And you will be surprised at....
And your unconscious mind can enable you to ...
And, in an interesting way, you'll discover...
Another part of you can take care of you comfort...
As that suggestion finds its mark...
At first..., but later....
At times like this, some people enjoy...
Before you (name outcome) you can always simply (another or related outcome)...
Can you notice...?
Continue by letting your unconscious...
During this relaxing yet profound process...
Enable a particular resource to surface...
Even though you THINK it would've been hard...

Mind Control Language Patterns

Find that these changes positively in your future...
Give yourself the opportunity to see if....
Have you begun to notice that yet?
I don't' know if you're aware of these changes, and it doesn't really matter.
I want to remind you of something that you probably already know, which is....
I want you to enjoy this experience.
I wonder if you'd like to enjoy...
I wonder if you'll be interested, in learning how, to...
I wonder if you'll be pleased to notice...
I wonder if you'll be reminded...
I wonder if you'll be surprised to discover that...
I wonder if you'll decide to ...or...
I wonder if you'll enjoy how naturally, how easily...
I wonder if you've ever noticed....
I would like you to appreciate the fact that...
I would like you to discover something...
I'd like you to begin allowing...
I'd like you to let yourself become more and more aware of....
In all probability....
If you could...
It is easy isn't it...
It may be that you'll enjoy...
It may be that you're already aware of...
It's so nice to know...
It's going to be a pleasure to ...
It's so easy, wasn't it?
It's very positive and comforting to know....
Just using the natural processes of your mind...
Keep changing in your life just like this...
Kind of like...
Maybe it will surprise you to notice that...
Now I'd like you to have a new experience.
Now of course I don't know for sure what you're experiencing , but perhaps you're...
Obviously, naturally, convincingly , now...
One of the first things you can become aware of is...
One of the things I'd like you to discover is...

Mind Control Language Patterns

Perhaps beginning to notice...
Perhaps even taking a special kind of enjoyment (in your ability to)...
Perhaps noticing...
Perhaps sooner than you expect...
Perhaps you wouldn't mind noticing...
Remember to forget to remember...
So just let it happen...
So now's the time...
So that it's almost as if ...
That ongoing commitment to change...
The learnings that are taking place...
The really important thing is just to be fully aware of....
The stuff reality is made of....
This makes sense like anything else in your life that you have totally accepted...
Very likely....
What's important, is the ability of your mind to....
When would NOW be a good time..
While another part of you really works to create this CHANGE NOW...
While you go to the proper level...
While YOUR UNCONSCIOUS continues to CREATE EVEN MORE POSITIVE CHANGE like this.
With you permission...
Wondering whether your unconscious will carry out this change or your conscious mind will..
You already know how to...
You don't need to be concerned if...
You'll be fascinated and feel a strong compulsion to ...
You might be fascinated and feel a strong compulsion to ...or to....

Mind Control Language Patterns

The Language Pattern That Frightened Psychologists:
Embedded Commands

You will hear many superlatives about this form of language pattern from those who have effectively used it. They will tell you embedded commands are simple to understand, wonderfully effective and difficult for others to detect. They will also tell you that embedded commands are easy to use, if you practice them.

Embedded commands are so effective that when first discovered and used by psychologists, they restricted teaching embedded commands only to licensed psychologists who were willing to pay several thousand dollars for the training. The fear was that embedded commands would fall into the wrong hands and be used by con-men and lascivious Lotharios.

The good (or bad) news is that the genie is out of the bottle, and embedded commands are now being taught to everyone, from salesmen to seducers.

Learning embedded commands is simple. Applying them demands some practice.

An embedded command is a single command that is hidden, or embedded, within a sentence. When used effectively, the command is clearly heard by the unconscious mind. This means that you can be speaking normally while these messages are being received, and the person will unconsciously follow the commands.

As an example, a normal sentence might be, *"I can see that you can get out from this a lot of benefit. You can leave your worries at the door."* The hidden messages are, *"Get out," "leave,"* and *"door."* You would find yourself unconsciously heading toward the door, if your unconscious mind only heard those words.

The key to making embedded commands work is to mark out the command, and make it different from the rest of the sentence.

To mark out the commands, the speaker needs only to pause before and after the command, and speak the command in a voice that is deeper, louder, or softer than the rest of the sentence. Using the annota-

Mind Control Language Patterns

tion of (...) to mean a pause and (**bold**) to mean a deeper tonality, the above sentence would sound like this:

> *"I can see that you can...**get out**...from this a lot of benefit. You can...**leave**...your worries at the...**door**."*

When the sentence is spoken intentionally in this manner, then they won't think anything about it, but *unconsciously*, their minds will hear the words *"Get out! Leave! Door!"*

You can be talking about *anything* when you are delivering your embedded commands, so think of the commands as the payload and the sentences that carry them as the stealth missile that delivers them.

Learning Embedded Commands

The most difficult part of embedded commands is simply putting the time aside to practice them. The following is an effective process for mastering this skill.

1. Choose your outcome.

Decide what you want the other person to do, and simplify it enough so you can put it into a simple phrase of less that four words.

Consider three different aspects of using embedded commands: the action, the feelings that motivate the actions, and the awareness of the person.

Assume you want the person to lean against the wall. What are simple commands that would describe that action? They could be "Lean," "Shoulder up," "Put your back into it," "Support the wall," "Rest against it," Get comfortable," "Rest."

Now, include commands and feelings that might motivate someone to do that. These feelings could be, "Put yourself at ease," "Relax," or "Feel Comfortable."

Include commands about what they might notice. "Notice the ease," "Notice the supporting pressure," "Notice how natural it is."

Your list might look like the following:

Lean

Mind Control Language Patterns

Shoulder up
Support the wall
Rest against it
Put your back into it
Rest
Put yourself at ease
Relax
Feel comfortable
Notice the ease
Notice the supportive pressure
Notice how natural it is

2. Choose the topic to contain the embedded commands.

Let's assume you are commanding the person to lean against the wall while describing the time you purchased a washing machine.

3. Place embedded commands into the topic, and mark them.

If new to this process, then you should write everything down the first few times, and make certain to mark out the commands using (...) to mean a pause and (**bold**) to mean a deeper tonality. Here is my example made up on the fly:

> *I just went to Acme Appliances and got a washing machine. When I get there I thought the salesman would really start to...**lean**...on me to buy, but instead, he really did...**shoulder up**...and make me...**feel comfortable**...so I wasn't...**up against a wall**...He made it seem as if you didn't have to...**put your back into it**...to find something you liked. The one I found was way in the...**back, resting against the wall**...It was a Washmate brand, the kind with the motto that says..."**Put yourself at ease**"...I wanted a good deal, so I tried something. I said "**Notice how natural it is**...to give me a discount," and he said he would...**do it**! And just like that, I...**lean back**...and...**notice the support**...they give their customers.*

4. Read it aloud - and _overdo_ the commands!

Mind Control Language Patterns

Yes, that's right, you must overdo them, and exaggerate your embedded commands far beyond what you think is normal. Make the pause (...) a one second pause. Make the **command** in a much deeper and/or louder voice.

You need to overdo and exaggerate the commands, in order to overcome this strange way of speaking. If you have never done embedded commands before, then it is likely you'll say your commands in the same way you speak, and the result will be zero impact on your subject.

Fear of Getting Caught Using Embedded Commands

There is a natural hesitation you will overcome when first using embedded commands. That hesitation comes from speaking in a new way. It will feel like you are sounding strange, and to you, you are. It is also the hesitation that someone who hears you speak will catch you.

The only people who could possibly notice you speaking "strangely" are those people who are used to how you normally speak. If they do notice you speaking differently, then rest assured, they will not know exactly what you're doing, only that it's different.

Mind Control Language Patterns

When I Talk About Me - I'm Talking About You
The I-You Shift

This is a very simple pattern, and something that we do all the time in regular conversation.

The I-You shift happens when one begins talking about their experience and moves from using the first person "I" to the second person "you." This is a covert way of telling someone to feel what you describe.

> *"I was thinking what happened to me yesterday. I was standing in line at the checkout counter, and someone asked me to hand them a magazine by the register. You know what it is like when someone looks at you and has such a kind voice and manner that you smile, and just do what this person says. And they just smile and tilt their head. It leaves you with such a warm feeling that you know it is something that you are going to remember for that day."*

In this example, the speaker is covertly telling the subject to feel a warm feeling toward them, using the I-You shift.

This one is fun and simple. Use the I-You shift in your next four conversations to create a feeling in someone that you want them to feel. All you have to do is start off by saying, "I had an interesting experience today. I..."

Mind Control Language Patterns

How To Compare Things, So That You Always Get What You Want
The Comparative Structure

Often people will have in their mind one thought, assumption or conclusion about something. They will have often abandoned any other alternative, as if they have discovered one flavor of cheese and forbid themselves to taste anything else.

On the one hand, this is reassuring, because they have landed solidly on their conclusion and no longer need to waste energy to think, analyze or consider anything else. On the other hand, they have forbidden themselves from the freedom of comparison.

What follows are various ways that one can introduce comparisons. They can be very simple - but they can be very trance inducing.

The As-As phrase

Here the word "as" is used twice to create an comparison.

"You'll find that you can notice your interest growing as easily as noticing the pleasure of a touch."

This sentence compares noticing "growing interest" to noticing "pleasure of a touch," and in so doing, links the two.

The Difference Between Pattern

"The Difference Between" pattern allows you to go into rich descriptive detail, describing two similar mental states. By describing these two states, X and Y, you covertly elicit them both.

To create a "Difference Between" pattern, ask yourself, "What mental-emotional states would drive someone to do what you want them to do?"

Upon determining what states would compel the action you desire, you then pose the question,

"Have you ever considered the difference between X and Y?"

Mind Control Language Patterns

What can make this pattern interesting is when X and Y are so similar that the difference between them has been overlooked, thus creating a sense of curiosity.

Attraction and Desire

"Have you ever considered the difference between attraction and desire?"

Attraction is when you begin to notice something in someone that you like. Perhaps it's just the fact that you laughed together, or that you feel comfortable enough to consider other things you want to do together. Attraction is when you have this person's face in your vision, even when they are not around.

Desire is something different, more intense. Desire has many of the qualities of attraction, of course, but you add to it a warmth that begins to pull you toward this person. I don't know if you notice it as a pull from the inside, or as if there is a force outside of you drawing you to this person, but you know it's happening, because somewhere in the back of your mind, you can hear this voice saying, "Mmm, yes! I gotta have that!" And it builds and builds and begins to take on a life of its own, so that no matter how much you try to suppress it, it just gets stronger."

Cost and Value

Most people are familiar with the credit card commercial that goes, "Wedding Ring: $1500. Wedding Dress: $2200. Bride's maids' gowns: $3200. A wedding she'll remember forever: priceless."

This pattern can be used in sales to emphasizes the value over the expense. "Have you ever considered the difference between what you're spending and the value of it and what you'll get with it. While the cost is $X, you'll get the priceless experience of (benefit) and (benefit) and (benefit)."

Want and Commitment

Mind Control Language Patterns

"Have you ever thought about what makes up the difference between want and commitment?

Want is interesting. You know that pull that comes from deep inside. You see your future out in front of you, and there is a chance that the thing you want might not be there. It's that feeling that might start as a piqued curiosity that says, "Yeah, I like that," and can turn into something so powerful that you almost find yourself screaming, *"I gotta have it!"*

Want is fast, frenetic and fun.

Commitment, on the other hand, is calmer and more solid. You can look out into your future and know beyond any doubt that what you want is there, and it's there because you decided, right now, to have it. There is no more want or pull. You simply did it and made it happen, and you did it because you knew it was the right thing to do."

Stillness and Immobility

"When you relax and get very comfortable, you may notice something that happens. You begin to make very subtle distinctions, and you can notice there is a difference between the comfort that causes a stillness and the difference between stillness and what it's like to become completely immobile, because you're so relaxed. With stillness, there is a calm that feels so comfortable that you don't need or want to move, and that stillness can grow stronger and stronger, until no matter what, you can't move, no matter hard you try."

Fear and Anxiety (Dark Pattern)

"You know some people don't really draw the distinction between fear and anxiety.

Maybe you remember what it's like to know something terrible is about to happen. It's like there is this ominous, heavy, dark figure, looming just behind you, out of vision, and you know if you turn around to check, that something painful and deadly will happen. Your heart pounds, and your breath is short and rapid. All you can do is run and hope that, by some small margin, you can escape it.

Anxiety is a type of fear, in its own right. Only this anxiety is that you know that something terrible and deadly is going to happen, and the worst part is that nothing that you can say will convince you that you're not going to die. No matter what you tell yourself, the terror only grows, and the walls being to shrink around you. The air gets thin, so you can only breathe in short gasps."

Depression and Hopelessness (Dark Pattern)

"There's a difference between depression and hopelessness.

I don't know how clearly you can imagine feeling so tired, all you want to do is go to sleep and not wake up. Maybe you're feeling sad about something that has happened. That's just one of the symptoms of depression. You can think of all that you've done in life, and realize that it doesn't mean anything; that there is nothing of any importance in life to think about, and all you can see within your mind is a vast, black emptiness. Nothing important is left to think about.

Hopelessness takes all your depression and places it everywhere in your future. No matter what you try to look forward to, it's not there. Just a black emptiness. All you can anticipate is that, no matter what happens, you can't be there to enjoy it. That part of you has been re-moved forever. Even now, you could feel every loss that you've experi-enced, as if they are all happening over and over again."

Mind Control Language Patterns

Getting To The "Core" Of Any Woman (or Man)
The Sacred Core Pattern

Consider that we all walk around with an outer persona that we present to the world. Also, at the same time, we protect another part of ourselves deep inside which holds our deepest desires and what we truly respond to.

They are not the same.
The outer persona holds all of our rules and roles within society.
The Sacred Core holds our deepest passions, hopes and dreams.

Originally used for seduction, the goal of this pattern is to get past the outer persona and to expose and touch the Sacred Core. Be warned. This is a powerful emotional pattern that exposes the vulnerability of the individual. If that vulnerability is mistreated, you will likely create an enemy who compulsively wants to hurt you. Imagine if someone else should mistreat the deeper self you share with them.

I find that, within most of us, there is a part that we all have to protect. You see, we go through life with this public self, and this public self is the part of us that has all the roles to play and all the rules to live by that we've all agreed upon. It even contains all the beliefs that we have about what we think we want.

But deep inside, there is another part that holds what we would truly respond to...things that we wouldn't even tell our closest friends. Within this very sacred core, we carry our hopes, our dreams, our fondest memories and our deepest desires. This part we protect, because it's where we hold things no one else knows.

It's also the place where anything can be possible. Where you can create and explore new feelings, new directions and even new behaviors that the outer persona protects from the world.

What I find is that it's rare to find someone who understands this part of you...this person...with whom you feel safe enough to...create an opening and invite them in, and there you can begin to explore together all the wonderful possibilities.

Mind Control Language Patterns

Doubt and Uncertainty Patterns

Doubt and uncertainty patterns are similar to sleight of mouth patterns, except they are not specifically designed to attack particular beliefs. Doubt and uncertainty patterns are designed to put the person into a state of willingness to consider alternatives.

Here are a sequence of doubt and uncertainty patterns, which can be used in any combination.

Are you sure?

This is just the beginning of patterning, and on a subtle level, it places the person in a position to question their certainty. Often it will yield a "Yes," as a reflex.

Are you sure you're sure - or just think you're sure?

"I think I'm sure."

That's right - you THINK so.

This response further distinguishes the difference between certainty and doubt.

Are you certain enough about X to be uncertain?

This puts the person into a double bind. If they answer "yes" then they are willing to doubt, and if they answer no then their certainty is not certain enough, and has doubt in it.

So you are certain about X? You know what it's like when you think something, but then you realize that you just think you think it? You go inside, and mentally, it gets turned around, so back is front, and what's left becomes right, and you realize that things aren't what you thought you thought they were.

Mind Control Language Patterns

This is a use of Ericksonian language, in order to induce doubt, and gently allow their mind to change.

Mind Control Language Patterns

How To Make Other Hear YOUR Voice in THEIR Heads
The Voice Of Experience Pattern

This is a very covert form of suggestion that comes from Ericksonian hypnosis.

Let's start by recognizing that, in one form or another, we all talk to ourselves. Sometimes we do it out loud, but more often, we have some sort of voice in our heads that we use to think, reason, rationalize and direct ourselves. For most people, this voice is a generic voice, with qualities no more distinct than the voice one hears when they speak.

What would it be like if you could make that inner voice in others' heads sound just like *your* voice? If someone were to wonder what to do, they would hear *your* voice talking to them. When wanting to encourage themselves, they would hear *your* voice cheering them on. Therefore, when they hear your voice over the phone or in person, it just feels right, because it's exactly like the voice in their heads. They would feel comfortable with almost anything you tell them.

"We all have memories of things we've learned, and maybe you can even remember your very earliest memory of learning, when you learned what it was like to learn. Maybe you were with a group of people or with someone older, but in that moment, you knew what it was like to learn, and everything seemed right. It sounded true, and it felt real.

In a lot of ways, it's like this voice - a voice of experience and support. So when you think about what it is you're going to learn, and you listen, you can hear this voice...and if you listen...really listen...you can hear this voice right now...speaking to you, right from the very center of who you are. This is your voice of experience and support. I have a voice like that, and you have this voice too...and even in the quiet moments of your thoughts, you can always hear this voice...guiding you, protecting you and keeping you from harm."

Mind Control Language Patterns

You'll note that there is nothing in this pattern that directly says, "My voice is the voice in your head," but when someone is hearing this pattern, at some level, they put in the speaker's voice as that "voice of experience."

There are a lot of ways you make variations of this pattern. One way is to simply ask, "Have you ever had to talk to yourself to get yourself motivated to do something?" And then ask what they would say to themselves, while consistently referring to "this voice" that makes them "go for it."

Have them play a game with you to put "this voice" in their head when they need it, and have them do things the instant they hear "this voice." Of course, you will practice being "this voice" for them. Secretly, you are training them to respond to *your* voice, by framing it all as a game.

Mind Control Language Patterns

How To Motivate People To Do ANYTHING You Want
Values Elicitation

When you find out what is most important to people, you can use it to influence and persuade them. The power of being able to do this is profound and can be used to help or harm.

The key is to uncover their set of values.

The good news is that it's much easier than you might think. Consider that people love to talk about what is important to them, when someone shows even a little interest. Sometimes, all you have to do is pay attention, and people will give you their hearts (more on this later). Other times, you only need to skillfully ask a few simple questions, and they will tell you everything you want to know about what motivates them.

Here is the process. First, understand that there is a context in which you want to influence the other person. This context could be selling a car, thus the context would be "cars." The context could be seduction, thus you would be talking about "romantic encounters." The rule is to keep the conversation within the context.

Once you are aware of the context, then the question you ask is quite simple. *"What's important to you about (context)?"*

So if the context is cars, then the question would be, "What's important to you about a car?" and if the context is sex, then the question would be, "What's important to you in a lover?"

A variation of this question can be, "When you have (context) fully and completely, what does that give you that's important?"

So, using the examples and this variation, the questions would be, "When you have the car you want, what does that give you that is important?" or, "When you have the lover or sex partner that you truly want, what does that give you that is important?"

When asking these questions, the first answer is not likely to be their deepest value, but it is important. In order to get to their deepest value for this context, you repeat the questioning cycle.

Mind Control Language Patterns

Let's say that your context is seduction, and you are attempting to woo a particular person. The first question asked is, "What's important to you in a lover?" Let us say they answer "romance." So to repeat this process, you would use the word "romance" as they have used it. "When you have romance fully and completely, what does that give you that's important?"

Let's then suppose the person's answer then becomes "passion."

This process of questioning would continue, until you reach their highest value. As a general rule, you will likely only have to repeat this process three times, sometimes less and sometimes more. How will you know their highest value has been reached? Pay attention, and look for some expression of emotion.

Keep in mind that these are people's highest values within this context, and for them to talk about it is bound to elicit emotions of some sort. This emotional response may be subtle or overt. It might not be tears, but you will want to pay attention to their response.

So, knowing that her first answer is "romance" and then "passion," you ask again. "What is ultimately important to you about passion?" Let's suppose their answer is "That would fulfill my deepest desire."

Keep in mind that we are only half way through the entire values elicitation process. Often this first half of the process of elicitation is enough for the person to begin to link these powerful values to you or your product.

Let's continue with the entire process.

Next, you use their answers to link their values to you or your product.

So you know that "romance" and "passion" are part of what makes their vision of an ideal partner and that ,ultimately, passion would "fulfill (her) deepest desire." All you do is work those exact words into the description of your values, or demonstrate them in your behavior.

You might later say something like, "When I think about the things that make a relationship worthwhile, there has to be a feeling of romance and passion, in order to fulfill my deepest desires," or "I don't know how well you can sit there and look at me as we talk, and know

Mind Control Language Patterns

that there is, deep inside, a sense of romance and passion that will be there to fulfill your deepest desire."

At first, this may sound mechanical and contrived, but keep in mind that you are talking about their highest values, and it has a very powerful effect.

This pattern is so powerful that it can influence people to do things they would not normally do.

Warning!!!

If this pattern is done to someone in a "dark" way, and they are persuaded to expect something you cannot live up to, then it is likely you will have made an enemy for life - or worse. You may have created someone who is compelled to hunt you down and kill you. Remember, this is manipulation on the level of a person's deepest values.

Mind Control Language Patterns

How to Destroy Old Beliefs and Install New Ones
The True/Used To Be True Pattern

The True/Used To Be True Pattern is very useful, if you want to help someone eliminate a limiting belief, and install a more supportive belief in its place. This pattern is also useful in various "dark" applications - but more on that, later in the book.

The True/Used To Be True Pattern works by altering how we view beliefs. As a general rule, we seldom examine our beliefs. Instead, we only notice how our beliefs affect us. For example, we feel dissatisfied, because want to do more with our lives, but there is a belief that holds us back that says, "I'm too old to learn anything new."

To use this pattern, you have to isolate the specific belief, and determine its positive and beneficial opposite. "I can learn anything," for example.

Once you have these components, the next step is to ask for two other thoughts that are unrelated to the belief you are going to change. These two new thoughts must both be absent of any strong emotions. These two new beliefs are, first, something you know that used to be true and second, something you know is absolutely true.

Having these two new thoughts, you need to find out the various qualities of them, what NLPers call *submodalities*. This means how they are pictured, their size, color and motion.

With this information, you would have them imagine the old unwanted belief that take on all the qualities of "something that used to be true," and the new and supportive belief that take on the qualities of something they know is true. What follows is a semi-dark conversational application of The True/Used To Be True Pattern.

Person A: Let me show you something about how your mind works. Think of something you know that used to be true for you, but it isn't any more. Something that isn't a big deal, like you used to ride a bike, but now you don't, or you used to be in high school, but now you aren't.

Person B: Okay, I've got it. I used to be in high school, but now I'm not.

Mind Control Language Patterns

Person A: When you think of how that used to be true, and picture it in your mind - could you point to where you see it in front of you? (Person B Points) What are it's dimensions? Is it in color or black and white? Is it still or in motion?

Person B: About 3 ft by 2 ft. in color. It's still.

Person A: Okay. Now, think of something you know is absolutely true - like you know the sun rises or that fire is hot - and tell me how it's is different.

Person B: Closer and right in front of me, and it's four feet by four feet. It's in color and in motion.

Person A: Great. Now let me show you something about how your mind works. Just suppose you looked in that area where something used-to-be-true, and right there, three feet by two feet, and in color, and still - is the image of you doubting what I have to tell you. Now, in that place where you put things that are absolutely true - see what I tell you, fitting in right there, and notice how it just fits NOW!

The effect is that you are covertly altering how they experience beliefs and that any doubt of what Person A says falls into used-to-be-true, and acceptance of what you say becomes absolutely true. Very devious, but useful, when you attempting to persuade someone.

It's important to note that to do something of this nature does require a great deal of rapport, and if you can add a sense of lighthearted fun to it, others will be more willing to follow along.

Working with an actual belief like, "I'm too old to learn" in a coaching or therapeutic setting is easier, because the other person is likely to know just what is going on and be willing to follow every step.

Mind Control Language Patterns

How To Make Yourself The Instant Expert
Credibility Patterns

These is a technique that helps add credibility and status to yourself. It is akin to name dropping, because it covertly links you to some expert or authority in your field. By so doing, you elevate your own status. Make sure the experts you use are relevant to the subject (don't quote an artist when you are talking about health care), and use experts that are alive. The covert expert endorsement goes like this.

"One thing I learned from (EXPERT'S NAME) was/is (WHAT YOU LEARNED FROM HIM/HER)."

Or

"If there was one thing that (EXPERT'S NAME) taught me, it's this: (WHAT YOU LEARNED)."

For example,

"One thing I learned from Steve Jobs is always innovate, never stagnate."

"If there was one thing that David Ogilvy taught me, it's this - always make your ads interesting. You can never bore people into buying from you."

As you can see, you don't have to actually know the person to have them covertly endorse you in this manner. This language patterns works best in writing when no one can ask you, "How do you know (EXPERT)?" Thus emails, ad copy and letters are the perfect medium.

It's best to use this language pattern cautiously when spoken, because it could be challenged and because excessive name dropping of this nature may be perceived as condescension and braggery.

Mind Control Language Patterns

Instantly Manipulate Your Social Status

Manipulating Social Status is not so much a language pattern as it is a process of subtly altering your behavior to influence people. For lack of a better term, the quality you will be affecting we'll call "status."

Status shows itself by the external demonstration of power between individuals. A person who is of high status will subtly demonstrate more power over others who have low status and, more importantly, the people of low status will respond.

So status is really about altering the relationship that exists between people.

A military general has more status than a private, and they demonstrate it in their behavior. They speak with more authority and in such a way that they know their commands will be followed.

A bouncer at a night club has status over everyone who wants in the club.

Many of us think that status is frozen and static, but it isn't. Suppose the private had a part time job working as a bouncer. In different situations, they would be interacting with the military general with differing levels of status, depending upon the situation. Because status is dynamic, one can alter it at will, instead of letting themselves be dominated by the situation or the social agreement.

A good example of the dynamic quality of status is that of a man asking for a date. If the man presents himself as lower status than the woman, he may feel she is "out of his league," and asking for a date might be a form of supplication. He might even say something like, *"You wouldn't want to go out with me on Saturday, would you?"* Were this man to present himself as equal or slightly higher status to the woman, he might instead say, *"Would you like to join me at the new comedy club opening this Saturday?"*

Status is a delicate thing. Too low a status, and you may be looked down on. Too high, and you may seem condescending. Status can be altered, depending on what you want to accomplish. To speak to a beautiful woman that a man has just met, it is often better to be of a status that is only slightly above hers. This allows a recognition of

Mind Control Language Patterns

equality but that he has more power and can thus provide more security and opportunity. This dynamic might change, when the two are in a romantic encounter, when his status is equal to hers.

In simple terms, people of high status don't physically move a great deal, because they have everything that they need, and they often have people who will do the actions for them. They don't even blink a great deal. The actor, Michael Caine, once described what happened when he learned about the concept of status. When rehearsing a character of high status, like a powerful mobster, he would practice speaking with a calm assurance, and do it so unblinkingly that people would begin to get intimidated or go into what seemed to him a hypnotic trance. He found that he could be very intimidating, even if he was calmly saying "You know, I like you Sonny. I really do. I don't want anything to happen to you."

Here are a list of behaviors and qualities of high and low status. These are the overt qualities that you can moderate, as you raise and lower your behavioral status.

High Status: calm, confident, secure

Low Status: nervous, worried, agitated

High Status: slow intentional movements

Low Status: twitchy

High Status: responsive, acting as if all reactions are planned and thought out.

Low Status: reactive, reflexive to what happens.

High Status: no blinking (not the same as staring)

Low Status: blinking with eyes darting

Being of high status may not always be the most effective strategy. To use the manipulation of status effectively, you must ask yourself what level of status would give you the best advantage in a given situation.

Mind Control Language Patterns

How To Control The Mind "Because" It's Easy
The Because Pattern

"This pattern is easy - because anyone can do it."

Quite simply, all you have to do is say "because" after almost anything you say, and offer some sort of reason. This works because the mind tends to accept anything as a reason simply because we say "because."

"This is an easy pattern to learn, because it was written in a book."

Now, I ask you, when you think about that sentence, what does having something "written in a book" have to do with it being easy to learn. Nothing! Yet, we tend to accept it as reasonable just...because. This is "because logic."

Other forms of "because logic" include:

- **due to** - *"Due to the fact that you're sitting down it's quite easy to feel comfortable and relax."*

- **for that reason** - *"We are all here in the same room, and for that reason it's not too hard to feel a little excitement."*

- **thus** - *"You're fairly nervous about attending the meeting, thus the whole prospect of giving the presentation can be fairly exciting."*

- **causes** - *"The lights are bright, and that causes you to focus on the beautiful decor of the living room."*

- **gives way to** - *"Knowing that there is a car parked outside gives way to an exciting feeling to escape this crazy party and have some real fun."*

Mind Control Language Patterns

- **yields** - *"The conversation yields an enthusiasm that makes following along easy."*

- **results in** - *"The fact that you're just here listening results in a sense of relaxation and an ease to hear more."*

(Dark Versions)

> *"You can probably notice that feeling of being stared at, because you're standing where everyone can see you."*

> *"It's natural for you to feel guilty, because you're standing in front of me."*

Begin to use this "because logic" in every situation you can think of, and notice how people will easily accept what you are saying. That's the power of "because logic."

Why does it work? Because!

Mind Control Language Patterns

How to Make Anything Mean Anything You Want
The X Means Y Pattern

As a rule, consider that, when you give a meaning to something, most people accept it, without question and that even bullshit sounds believable, when spoken congruently. This is a power that con-men bring to their nefarious craft; because they speak congruently, as though they believe themselves, they gain "confidence" with others that they are speaking the truth.

Please note that we all use this form of deception in everyday life. Much like the example of the "Because Pattern," the "X means Y" pattern is both simple and powerful. To use this pattern, one says that one thing means another thing.

Here are some examples:

"The fact that you're here means you're going to listen in on some important information."

"Standing in this room shows your sincere interest to learn more. I deeply respect that."

"There is a strong implication that you're interested in me, just by the kind way you hand me the papers."

"That you are sitting so close indicates you are going to learn a lot from this process."

Here are some darker examples:

"That you are willing to speak about it so calmly is a sign of the incredible guilt you're going to feel when you are revealed as a fraud."

"If you have a bad dream it means you're did something wrong that only confession will absolve."

Mind Control Language Patterns

How to Bind Your Success
The Single Bind Pattern

The Single Bind pattern works in the same way as "because logic." People just tend to accept it, without question. Simply put, the single bind pattern links an action to a feeling.

The simplest construction of the single bind is, "The more you X - the more you Y," but it can be morphed in a number of ways:

"The more you watch, the more curious you'll become."

"The more you think about it, the more interesting it becomes."

"The sooner you agree, the faster you'll feel satisfied."

"The faster you do it, the less you will hurt."

"The less you resist, the more you'll enjoy."

"The more you study, the more you'll remember it."

"The more you sweat in training, the less you bleed in combat."

"The faster you act and the less you think, the more quickly you'll enjoy the suggestion."

"The slower you eat, the more you'll enjoy the taste and texture of the food."

Here are some darker examples:

"The more you worry about your erection, the harder it will be to get one."

"The more you interrupt me, the more guilt and shame you'll suffer."

"The more you think about that embarrassment, the more painfully humiliating it becomes for you."

Mind Control Language Patterns

Choosing Between Two Evils is Still Choosing Evil
The Double Bind Pattern

A Double Bind pattern creates a choice in the other persons mind - and either choice will give you what you want. A typical example of a double bind is being asked by a cashier whether you want to pay with cash or credit. The bottom line is that you will pay, thus the refusal of either option still creates the same result.

A double bind combined good rapport will minimize the amount of antagonism felt when offered to pick the lesser of two evils. The doctor asked, while smiling, "Do you want the hypodermic injection in the arm or the hip?" Either way - you got a shot.

Also, you will get stronger results by adding emotional responses into your double binds. Here are some examples:

"When you consider how comfortable you feel, you can either linger on it to get the most from it, or you can begin to imagine how much more real pleasure is possible."

Also:

"Sitting here a person can either just sit back and relax, or they can get comfortable with everything around them."

Here are some darker examples:

"You can either think about what you did and how it hurt people, or you can let the guilt build up and haunt your every waking moment." Also, *"When that feeling of anxiety automatically appears you can either let it grow stronger or you can think about how much stronger it will grow no matter what."*

Mind Control Language Patterns

How To Double the Impact, Seal The Deal
& Lock In The Emotions You Want:
Meta States

The central key to understanding meta states is to know the difference between a "primary state" and a "meta state." A primary state is a thought or feeling. For example, *"I feel sad"* is the statement of a primary state. To think about a concept like death is a primary thought.

A meta state is a thought or feeling *about* thoughts or feelings. For example, *"I feel guilty about my sadness"* describes a state - in this case, guilt, about a primary state - in this case, sadness.

Likewise, thinking about thoughts of death would also be a meta state. *"I think it would be interesting to think about death."*

One can take a single state, sadness for example, and associate many meta states to it. A person can feel fear about their guilt about their sadness, and thus have two levels of meta states, fear and guilt. As you can see, this example describes a very uncomfortable state, where someone can be trapped into a cycle of sadness, the primary emotional state.

As an alternative, one can start with the same emotion of sadness and go in a different direction with the meta states. They can feel sadness, then relief about their sadness, and then finally joy about their relief. So imagine feeling joy about your relief about your sadness. It's quite a different experience.

In this way, meta states can be suggested, in order to achieve an end result, but starting with any originating primary state. To "lock in" the new meta state, all one has to do is to ask the subject to notice the original primary state.

Consider the following exercise:

Either alone or with a partner, begin with an originating state X.

Now ask,

"When you notice X, what thoughts or feelings come to mind?"

or,

Mind Control Language Patterns

*"How do you feel **about** X?"*

In this way, you will get the meta state, because it is a state that is one level removed from the primary state. Ask the same question, even further. "When you notice that feeling about X, what thoughts or feelings do you then have?"

You can also suggest meta states, such as saying, *"As you notice that uncertainty (the primary state), can you bring to bear a calm sense of relaxation, and notice how that feels?"* In this case, the person feels uncertainty and then a sense of calm.

As a "dark application," consider the same person feeling uncertainty and then being asked, *"As you notice that uncertainty and it grows, notice how it overlaps anxiety."*

Notice that, by asking questions in this way, it continues to distance the subject from their original state. This is why, if you want to connect the person to the new meta states, you must reconnect them to the primary state.

Mind Control Language Patterns

How To Make People Crazy
Gaslighting

Gaslighting is the process of causing someone to doubt their own thoughts, beliefs and perceptions. The term "gaslighting" come from the 1944 movie "Gaslight," about a man who attempted to cause his wife to go crazy by making her doubt what she was seeing.

To understand gaslighting, you must realize that it happens all the time and that it is a basic process of human communication. Gaslighting, in itself, is neither good nor bad. Like many of these patterns, it is how they are applied that make them a light or dark pattern.

Sometimes gaslighting is done effectively and our subject willingly reevaluates what they are perceiving, and other times we do it with a brute force, by telling people, "You're wrong." As you might guess, this latter technique is minimally effective. The point is that gaslighting is a central aspect of human communication.

When someone is willing to rethink their thoughts, perceptions and conclusions, they are much more open to suggestion.

Gaslighting Method #1: Repeated Questioning

One way to cause people to reevaluate what they are sensing is to ask a series of questions that cause the subject to analyze things about the topic that they weren't focusing on. Doing this in a supportive fashion only encourages the subject to follow through with the process. At the conclusion of the questioning, the subject may be completely confused about what they had thought or seen.

Consider what happens when you are repeatedly asked to explain something. Each time, there is subtle variation in the story, and we can soon begin to doubt our own thinking.

It is in this way that police find failures in stories and even get false confessions. This process has been documented to be used in unethical police interrogations in which the subject is lead from, "What did you do?" to "Could you have done..." to "You said it was possible you could have done it. Are you sure you didn't?" - to a complete signed confession.

A classic example of how repeated questions are used as a gaslighting technique can be witnessed by watching most any documentary that is made by Paranoid Conspiracy Theorists (PCT). During these documentaries you will often be posed questions that are never answered but leave you thinking in the direction that the documentary makers want you to go.

You may hear a string of questions like this:

"How can we know that these explanations are true?"

"Could it be there is something else going on?"

"How can the so-called experts explain these apparent contradictions?"

"What else is going on that they are hiding?"

"Are we truly safe from other possible deceptions?"

By asking these questions and not answering them, the viewer is lead to question their own perceptions and assumptions. Very tricky stuff.

The light use of this pattern is to ask questions that focus a person's attention away from sadness, failure, disappointment, and toward a more positive direction. The pinnacle of gaslighting techniques is sleight of mouth, which will be discussed in more detail later. Sleight of mouth is a questioning process that specifically causes a reevaluation of ones' beliefs.

Gaslighting Method #2: Pointing Out The Invisible

When there are things that we don't perceive around us, it's natural to question what we are perceiving. An example of that is when a doctor or some other professional begins to point out the significance of certain personality traits of which we are not aware. Because these traits are not within their awareness, the person will tend to halt their judgment and accept the reality that is given to them.

Mind Control Language Patterns

Light use of this technique is done by pointing out positive traits and gives the individual a heightened sense of self. Likewise, the dark use of this pattern would be to describe destructive traits in a manner that implies that they are uncontrollable, and therefore they will persist.

Gaslighting Method #3: Alluding To The Mysterious

This form of gaslighting is similar to pointing out the invisible. It is simpler, because it can employ a familiar tactic - bullshit. By calling someone's outburst or hesitation a "complex," it creates a sense of authority and dependence on the person who describes the "complex." By doing this, many people discover the value of nonsense.

Gaslighting Method #4: Revealing the Secret Thoughts of Others

Imagine yourself in the following scenario.

You are part of a close knit social group and feel a strong rapport with the group and all the people in it. You are liked by others for your good humor, and you often regale them with jokes that leave them laughing. To your knowledge, everything is going well, and the world is running in greased grooves.

You are then taken aside by one of the people closest to you, and it is revealed that the majority of the group finds your jokes pedantic and boring. He further tells you that the group is concluding that you must be an idiot, because you seem to refuse to notice their annoyance each time you begin your one man stand up comedy routine. He then asks you to not return to any more of the groups social gatherings.

Given that experience, most people would begin to reevaluate what they first thought about their sense of humor. To turn this into a language pattern, start with, *"They wouldn't want you to know I told you..."* or *"Please, don't let X know that you heard this from me,"* and then follow with whatever the "secret thoughts" would be.

"Don't tell your boss I told you, but he told me your presentation made all the difference in choosing to increase your team's funding. He actually told me you turned him completely around."

"You seem very eager to be a part of our team. I hate to be the one to tell you this, but your comments have not been welcomed. They

side track the topic and have annoyed enough people that, if you don't shut up and listen, they won't be taking part at all."

Gaslighting Method #5: Social Pressure

This one has a long history of research behind it. In brief, it states that social pressure is very hard to resist. Social pressure can easily alter our actions, but it can also cause us to change our perceptions.

The skillful and artful way to apply social pressure is to do it gradually. Design the group to have its own secret agenda for the newcomers. They are to be kept happy and gradually led in the specific direction that is designed for them. The best way to do this is to plan ahead and have everyone play their part.

Keep in mind that this is done all the time in schools, churches, cults, fraternities and families and happens regardless of whether the intent is benevolent or malicious.

Mind Control Language Patterns

Know The Weakness of Any Man (or Woman)
Hidden Addictions

"Hidden addictions" were first described by Blair Warren in his book and e-course called "The Forbidden Keys of Persuasion."

These "hidden addictions" are, in fact, seven needs to which we all respond. The term "addiction" is used, because these needs are so powerful that we respond to them almost as if they were drugs. They are so strong that we respond to them even when we know they are being used on us.

As language patterns, these hidden addictions are more difficult to qualify as either light or dark. They are simply factors to which people naturally respond.

Hidden Addiction #1: The need to be needed.

Consider that everyone positively responds to knowing that they are needed, appreciated and valued. As a language pattern, it is very easy to enlist someone using this technique. Here is a six-step process that can be used as a guideline to employ this hidden addiction.

1. Explain the situation as a whole. What is at stake? What is the dilemma?

2. Explain the specific role the person can play in the situation.

3. Emphasize the importance of the role.

4. Point out how the person is uniquely qualified for the role.

5. Openly acknowledge that your request will require a sacrifice on their part.

6. Ask if you can count on them to help.

Using this technique takes hardly any time at all.

"Mark, the project is reaching the deadline - and it's going to be close. If we don't make it, we'll lose out on any more contracts of this

nature - and you're the one person with the technical skills to complete it. To get it done, it'll take a some extra hours. Of course, you'll be compensated for the time, but the important part is getting it done. You're a vital part of this project. Can we rely on you?"

The Black Ops use of this hidden addiction would be in getting someone to do something (or not do something) that would be detrimental to them.

Hidden Addiction #2: The need for hope

When aware of an impasse, people will do anything to gain a sense of hope. This one is very common sense. Anyone in a tough situation will respond to anything that gives them hope. As a dark tactic, one might secretly create a problem for someone, or put them in a state of confusion, and then give them relief from their difficulty and confusion.

Hidden Addiction #3: People need a scapegoat

The reason this hidden addiction is so powerful is that it is much easier to blame someone or something else than to look inside and find out how we might be responsible. To blame something else means to seriously reevaluate what we are doing, and even our own perceptions.

As a language pattern, this hidden addiction can be reduced to four words, *"It's not your fault."* But any time you offer an explanation for a problem, other than blaming the sufferer, you've fulfilled this hidden addiction. People will respond to it, even if it isn't true.

Hidden Addiction #4: The need to be noticed and understood

While this can be a language pattern, it does not have to be. Anything that allows people to feel noticed is important. The simplest way to make people feel understood is through "active listening," which is to rephrase what they say, and ask for acknowledgment. You don't have to agree with them, because that isn't the point. Simply acknowledge that you hear what they say by restating it.

Mind Control Language Patterns

Hidden Addiction #5: People need to know what they aren't supposed to

"Allow me to let you in on a very sneaky and DANGEROUS secret."

Just hearing those words, people will involuntarily lean forward and listen. Why? Because having a secret makes someone special and implies extra knowledge and power, which that secret endows.

To use this hidden addiction as a language pattern, all you have to do is work in these words and phrases into the information you're providing: *prohibited, banned, closed, closed down, closed up, contraband, no no, off limits, outlawed, proscribed, refused, taboo, verboten, vetoed, confidential, closely guarded, eyes only, top secret, illegal, black market, banned, bootlegged, exclusive, prohibited, illicit, clandestine, back room, no-fly zone, restricted, ruled out, unacceptable, unmentionable, unthinkable.*

Hidden Addiction #6: People need to be right

People need to be right...even if they are wrong. The reason this is such a powerful addiction is that, for them to admit they are wrong, they would have to question their own perceptions and assumptions. To call them wrong, as mentioned above, would be a very ineffective form of gaslighting.

If they are wrong, and you have to correct them anyway, then your best option is Hidden Addiction #3 - give them a scapegoat. In other words, you will tell them, "You're wrong, but it's not your fault (scapegoat). You just didn't know."

Hidden Addiction #7: People need a sense of power

There are no good feelings in being powerless. If given the chance to feel in control, people will always respond positively. To make someone feel in control and as if they have power, the simplest way is to give them the final choice in something.

In his book, The Forbidden Keys to Persuasion, Blair Warren described talking to a woman whose daughter was becoming part of a cult, and she was concerned and had expressed her objections to her daughter's involvement. Blair explained what the cult leader is likely to say to her daughter.

Mind Control Language Patterns

"Of course your family loves you. They only want the very best for you. At some point, Jennifer, you're going to have to make an adult decision as to what you need to do. Of course we'd love you to be with us, but the choice is really yours. No one can make that decision for you."

Given her mother's pressure to leave the cult and the cult telling her it's her choice, it's easy to see that the cult is giving her a sense of power.

Mind Control Language Patterns

How To Open The Door To A Woman's Heart
The Emotional Chamber
(as created by JD Fuentes)

The "emotional chamber" is a language pattern that has wide application, when working with women. It creates a metaphor for the female sexual response, and here are its components:

Step 1. Create a doorway or opening where an emotion can be brought in.

Step 2. Create kinesthetic descriptions of the emotion, such as "warm," "tingling" or "electric."

Step 3. Escalate the feeling, culminating to a peak or climax of the feeling.

Step 4. The culmination yields to different feelings that are brought in, and the cycle begins again.

"When a person finds that they are interested in XYZ, it's often like you have to stop and create an opening, like a doorway, and bring in a sense of curiosity. Now, as you bring in that tingling curiosity, it can begin to grow and build, until finally, it culminates in a feeling of sincere interest. So you welcome in this feeling of interest, and it goes in very deep, and the interest takes on a warm and welcoming feeling that grows stronger and stronger and stronger, until it explodes into this feeling of want...so you welcome in this electric feeling of want, and it begins to intensify and build, until it gets so strong that finally, finally...FINALLY you realize this XYZ is yours - and you're going to get it."

Mind Control Language Patterns

Why Ask - When You Can Tell Them What To Do?
The Zero Decision Pattern

The Zero Decision Pattern removes the other person's choices, by simply not offering them one.

When decisions need to be made, the individual first has to have some understanding of what they are deciding. This understanding can act as a barrier to their taking action, so it is often better to make it so that they don't have to choose or decide.

For example, if Mr. J. is given a choice between X and Y, then he will have to make a mental effort to decide. The Zero Decision Patterns simply removes the choice. So instead of asking, "Would you like to go ahead with the program?" and giving him a choice between saying "yes" or "no," you might say, "Let's step over to the schedule, and see where you can fit in" or, "The program you'll be in starts on Monday."

When Mr. J. tells you what he wants, it is important that you tell him he is right for wanting it. That will only make him want it more (people love to be right). Then tell him what to do next. Don't ask. Tell!

So Mr. J. wants service X but can't afford it. First, agree with him for wanting it. "Mr. J, you want X. You're right to want it. Your program starts...," or "Good choice. Here is the program package you'll be using." If Mr. J says, "I don't have the funds," reply, "Good. Bring what you can, and we'll setup payments. Be here on..."

If you are putting the zero decision pattern into effect for your business (it's a damn good idea), then you must drill into every employee to direct the client and never to ask. It is also good to write these patterns into the conversational patter your employees are taught to use when dealing with the public.

The tone of voice is important, in order to avoid feeling bullied, so consider how you might say it, if you were ordering from a menu, with a kind smile on your face.

The unique part of this pattern is that, with ongoing exposure, a person will automatically get used to following the commands. Why wouldn't they? They are simple and not really a choice - just what they are supposed to do!

Mind Control Language Patterns

To summarize the Zero Decision Pattern:

- Find out what they want and why, and agree that they are right and good to want it.
- Tell them (don't ask) the very next step and direct them. Don't tell them they need to, and don't offer options. Just tell them to do it. Consider saying it like you were ordering from a menu. No emotion just direction.
- Avoid making a big deal out of your direction. Say it as if it's what everyone does.

Mind Control Language Patterns

Lead Others Through Confusion: Confusion Patterns

Confusion is a very uncomfortable feeling, which people will do almost anything to avoid, even if it means accepting the next thing you tell them as the truth. This tendency makes confusion a very useful tool of influence. In other words, create confusion and offer the solution.

The simplest way to induce confusion is the non-sequitur.

People operate within the boundaries of certain sequences or patterns. If right now your computer transformed into a singing turnip, you will likely be at a complete loss about what to do. You would quickly retreat into a deep hypnotic trance, while your mind tries in vain to make sense of the situation.

The same is true of the non-sequitur. By saying something meaningless and totally unexpected, while stating it with the air of something meaningful and important, people will retreat into a momentary trance to try and understand what you said. This confusion gives you time to quickly slip in a command, and be delighted as you see it followed through.

When stating a non-sequitur, it's important that it appears you are doing nothing unusual. They will assume there is meaning in what you say and will search inside, in order to figure it out.

Here is an example in sales:

Customer: *"You know, I don't think this computer is for me."*

You: *"Fortunately, clouds don't fall from cars."*

Customer: (blank expression while he or she processes your statement)

You: *"Funny how easy it is to change your mind, isn't it? I used to think I didn't like soccer, but then found that I loved it. You may soon realize that the same is true of this computer."*

Here are some other non-sequiturs:

"The wall outside my house isn't four feet tall."

"The clock I don't have doesn't say it isn't seven-thirty."

Mind Control Language Patterns

"The list of night is running back, isn't it?"

My personal favorite, which induces an instant state of confusion is,

"Consider what you are not thinking right now."

The important point is that, as soon as the other person enters a state of confusion (i.e. trance), you must be prepared to instantly offer something that they can hold on to, like how good your product is or how good they feel.

Mind Control Language Patterns
Fun Playing With People's Emotions:
The Art Of Anchoring

"Anchoring" is the name that NLP (neuro-linguistic programming) has given to the mind-control technique of classical conditioning. Basically, you are adding bias and emotion to a situation, which then influences the person's perception. By changing the emotion that a person perceives within a situation, they are much more likely to alter their behavior. When anchoring is used correctly, it becomes very easy to unconsciously control other people...in both a good and bad way.

You can anchor pleasant wonderful emotions, like joy and excitement, and link them to some action or object, so that people go after them. You can also anchor painful and negative emotions, and link them to objects and activities, so that people avoid them. This is one powerful technique indeed!

It is important to understand that anchors are being created all the time - unintentionally. When we are in a bad mood in a certain location, we tend to not want to return to that location, because the bad mood is anchored to the location.

A Little Background To Classical Conditioning

In psychology class, you may remember classical conditioning and Pavlov's dog. Put simply, classical conditioning is when your brain pairs things together that happen at the same time. For example, the sound of opening a can of soda will probably make you also imagine a carbonated, cold drink. Picking up the remote control will probably remind you of watching television.

It is also very common for unrelated things to be paired together in your brain. For example, you may have had a romantic relationship in the past, and your lover always smelled of a particular perfume. The thought of your lover brings back memories of desire and passion. Because of classical conditioning, the smell of that fragrance may also bring you feelings of desire and passion. By itself, perfume fragrance has nothing to do with desire and passion, but your brain has paired all of these things together.

Mind Control Language Patterns

Perfume fragrance -> Previous Lover -> Desire and Passion
Perfume fragrance -> Desire and Passion

The famous Pavlov rang a bell, when he fed a dog. After the dog had been conditioned, or "anchored," the dog salivated, when he rang the bell.

Ring Bell -> Get Food -> Salivate
Ring Bell -> Salivate

The Significance Of Pairing Unrelated Things

There are two ways of using the technique of anchoring. The first is to observe your subject, in order to find out things that they have feelings about (an activity, a relationship). Once you've identified a topic that elicits a response, you can then pair a new stimulus to the topic. The second way is to elicit the feeling from them (more on this later).

Bill really likes to watch football games. When he talks about football, his eyes light up, and he becomes very animated and passionate.

Football -> Excitement & Enthusiasm

So now, during your conversation with Bill, you are going to anchor another thing (snapping your fingers) to football. So now every time that you mention football, you snap your fingers. When John mentions football, you also snap your fingers. With enough repetition, Bill will eventually pair you snapping your fingers with the idea of football.

Snapping your fingers -> Football

Once Bill has made this pairing, you will now have the ability to trigger the excitement and enthusiasm inside him, whenever you want.

Snapping your fingers -> Football -> Excitement & Enthusiasm

Snapping your fingers-> Excitement & Enthusiasm

Lets pretend that you want Bill to like your friend Jane. So while talking to Bill, you snap your fingers, and begin describing Jane

Mind Control Language Patterns

to him. Unconsciously, Bill will feel excitement and enthusiasm, and his perception of Jane will have this bias. Now when you introduce the two, Bill is much more likely to have the emotions of excitement and enthusiasm for Jane. It works.

The Steps to Anchoring Any Emotional Response

1. Find what creates an emotional response (hate, fear, love, disgust, embarrassment).

2. Attach a trigger (snapping your fingers, flaring nostrils, grab your ear) by using repetition.

3. Use the trigger to elicit the emotional response.

Testing your success is a matter of paying close attention to your subject, in order to notice their response.

Eliciting Emotional States

There are several ways to elicit the emotional state you want to anchor in someone. You can have them talk about what brings up that emotion. Just asking, *"Have you ever been in love? What is that like for you?"* will tend to bring up a feeling of love. *"What was the saddest event you've ever had?"* will bring up sadness and depression.

Another way is to describe the emotional state to them, and lead them into it. This method can be a bit harder, because the state you describe may not perfectly fit how they would feel the same emotion.

The Game of Anchoring Drunkenness

This game involves elicitation and anchoring. It's quite fun and should be always presented as a game, to get the best involvement from people.

The first thing is to work with someone who remembers what it feels like to be drunk. Ask your volunteer to describe what it's like, starting with the first sip and how they feel the earliest buzz of alcohol. This is the elicitation process.

Mind Control Language Patterns

After the state is elicited, have them mentally go over the state again and again, amplifying it, until they are acting as if they are drunk.

The anchor can be anything, so I often recommend you use a unique word on a small card. While in their self-created drunken state, hold up the card, and have them look at it. The next step is to have them "sober up," and get them fully out of the drunken state. Have them walk a straight line, to demonstrate that they can do it, without trouble. Then have them do it again, but this time hold up the card with the word on it - and watch them begin to stumble.

The point of this game is to both have fun and to practice the elicitation and anchoring processes. Have fun!

The Game of Anchoring Catalepsy

This is much like the above game and is done in a climate of lightheartedness.

It starts with the basic setup of *"Can I show you something fun about how your mind works?"* and can easily follow the Anchoring Drunkenness game.

First, you get the agreement that, to do this, you have to make sure that they can notice an emotional or mental state that they are in, and hold it for a while. So you have them go through a list of fun and benevolent emotions, such as joy, glee, lightheartedness, wonder, curiosity - and each time they get into that state, you touch them on the arm or shoulder (a physical anchor), and say *"Hold it. Stay there."* (auditory anchor). You do this, until they demonstrate that they are good at holding that state.

You then ask them a questions that elicit an internal sense of confusion, and anchor it, by touching them with the physical and auditory anchor.

Some examples of the questions you ask could be, *"What are you not thinking right now?"* or *"I wonder what the next thought you have will be."*

What makes this trick amusing is that you leave them in that state.

Mind Control Language Patterns

Influence Their Hearts and Minds:
Emotional Elicitation Patterns

Warning...

In order to make the point of how emotions are used to persuade, I have two outcomes in mind. The first is to demonstrate subtle emotional elicitation. The second is to encourage you to invest in learning more about Mind Control Language Patterns. Yes, I am being overtly manipulative. I AM! Because, in order for persuasion to occur, it must happen within a context. The context is: Learning Mind Control Language Patterns.

Emotions

When first learning persuasion skills, it's often the goal of the initiate to make people do certain things that are in the initiate's interest. They may consider simply putting the subject in a trance and telling them to do things for them. That is rare, and the learner of persuasion will quickly find out that people are not motivated by thoughts, but by emotions. It is through the elicitation of emotions in the subject that the persuader will get their outcome.

In persuasion literature, they are referred to as "discrete emotions," because they are elicited and felt subjectively, without an outward expression. Most persuasive writing and speeches appeal to several emotions, both positive and negative. When you read a persuasive sales letter, you can begin to list the emotional states they are trying to elicit. Likewise, when you are persuading someone, be mindful of their emotional states and the emotions you are trying to elicit.

I'd like to demonstrate, in writing, the persuasive use of both *positive* and *negative* emotions.

The Need to Learn Mind Control Language Patterns

Pride - Let me first begin by saying, "Thank you." Of all the people in the world, you've taken the steps that have brought you here to learn more about persuasion. That translates as you being a single fraction of a percent of all the people in the world who value themselves enough to know that learning persuasion skills is absolutely *vital* to your success and well being. Before you read any further, take a second to acknowledge your efforts in getting this far, because there are too many moments that pass us by, when we don't take pride in what we've done.

Fear - I've been studying persuasion for almost a decade, and the sad fact is that there are some people who know these skills and would use them on anyone, regardless of the possible negative effect it might cause. Some people have referred to these as "Dark Side" NLP skills, and I can tell you from personal experience that they *do* exist! I also know that the only way to protect yourself from any of these malicious processes and language patterns is to know about them. Yes, knowledge is your only defense against the most wicked people who would even think to use them.

Anger -I've seen the results of these destructive language patterns. They are devious, because most people don't even know they've happened. They live life half-heartedly, with no purpose, because *someone meant to hurt them*! If you know of anyone using these language patterns and NLP skills to injure, you have every right to act and stop them!

Hope -But there is a bright side to all of this. Persuasion skills like the ones I teach are there to *benefit* you and everyone who knows them. Using these skills, I've seen people overcome life-long phobias, and land million dollar contracts. You can use these skills just as easily to land the perfect job, meet your ideal romantic partner and end what may at times seem like an endless cycle of just trying to pay the bills. Knowing these persuasion skills and how to apply them, you can benefit your life and the lives of others.

Envy - Okay, it's true we want all of that. What sane person doesn't? I have a friend who easily uses the persuasion skills I teach to get everything he wanted. He's happy, he's loved, he's proud of what he's accomplished, and every time we meet, he's eager to tell me, or anyone, about the richness that life has to offer. He also wants everyone to know that they can have what they want, too. Some people will tell you that he's a

Mind Control Language Patterns

freak, an abnormally happy person, but his message is that he got it largely due to his hard work and knowledge of how the mind works. For him, persuasion has become easy.

Guilt - He has a less positive side, too. There are some times when he's taken people aside and reminded them how much they haven't really lived up to what they could do. He makes a good point. We each may have started with an idea or ideal, but we stopped and never finished it. There is something to be said about squarely facing your shortcomings.

You may have shown an interest in persuasion - but how much have you really dedicated yourself to learning and using it. For most people, the answer is *"Not much."* When you're faced with that reality, it can really eat away at how you think of yourself. That's a burden I don't want you to ever face again.

Sadness - It can be like we've really lost something. Lost a hope for our lives. By realizing that we haven't lived up to what we could be, most people are compelled to act. Compelled to do something... anything, rather than feel the real burden and misery of losing control of life.

Happiness/Joy -The one great comfort of all of this is that there is a solution that comes by just taking a few simple steps. One of them is making a decision to learn persuasion skills by investing in your first product. When you do that, you know you're doing something right. Improving yourself is the one act no one can take away, and it will be with you for the rest of your life.

Relief - When you do take those steps, a burden will be lifted. If you could imagine the freedom of having the time to enjoy the things that you want, take vacations and participate in the social activities you've always loved, that's what you'll have for yourself, by becoming a life-long student of persuasion skills.

Anticipation -You've read this far, so I know you're showing some interest - and there is a lot to look forward to. Think about it. Instead of looking back on what you could have done but didn't, you can start to look forward to making life-changing decisions.

Let me paint a picture for you of what you can look forward to when you become a master of Mind Control Language Patterns. First, you will have fun, you'll enjoy the adventure of power, and you will also become free, absolutely free, of all the weaknesses that came when you were lost and impotent. Free from hurt. Nothing to regret. As you learn these skills, your life will change, as well. You'll find that you're more confident, relaxed and able to talk to anyone, anytime.

Regret - My friend, Tony Robbins, points out that, near the end of life, most people find it way TOO easy to look back, and see the opportunities we could have chosen but didn't. It's the things we didn't do that we regret more than what we choose to do. There is an opportunity right now that could change everything for you...and you could pass it up, and regret it forever.

Let me just stop right here, and point out that no one really knows how much time we have on this earth. Because we don't know, we think it's limitless, but it's not. You have no idea how many full moons you'll see in your life - maybe twenty, maybe only five. How many times will you see a butterfly spread its wings and fly? Maybe ten times? Maybe less. Maybe more.

Opportunities are like that too.

When you commit yourself, you've made the decision that will positively affect you and everyone around you. Don't walk away, and make a choice to live only half a life.

Every moment is an opportunity, and using your knowledge of persuasion, you'll be able to take advantage of opportunities you never knew how before.

Conclusion

The list of emotions used is by no means exhaustive, and I encourage you to explore how to use discrete emotional appeals to persuade, influence and negotiate.

Let me first recognize that a few readers may have read this far and felt unnerved, irritated or coerced and even compelled to invest in persuasion products. That is not the point. Emotions play a powerful part in any persuasion context, no matter how subtle. It will benefit any would-be persuasion expert to pay attention to the emotions they see and the emotions they attempt to elicit.

Mind Control Language Patterns

Mind Control Language Pattern Example

The following is a personals ad that uses all various patterns already discussed. The ad has been tested by submitting it to free "men searching for women" personals forums in various cities, to measure the response. It has consistently gotten SOME interesting replies. There was no follow-up to the replies; the exercise was to measure only if women would favorably respond to it, and they did..

Please note how this personals ad says virtually NOTHING about the author, while eliciting strong emotional responses.

What am I like?

Before you read any further, I want you to notice something interesting about yourself. It's that feeling of curiosity. It's that warm, compelling feeling that makes you focus in a little deeper or move a little closer, to find out what you want to know.

I'm a lot like so many people you've known and felt that curious feeling of familiarity, that "click" that tells you that you're in for something interesting.

At this point, you might think, at some level, that you may know me - and in a sense, that would be true. There are men just like me you pass by every day - some you acknowledge, some you don't even remember. Some, like me, want to look you in the eyes and shake you, telling you "Wake up! Do you know what you are missing right this very moment?"

There is something within you that only a few men have known, but something you want to share. The problem is that this "something" you have to keep safe and protect. It's that part of you where you keep your hopes and dreams and secret desires... those things you wouldn't even tell your closest friends. Most men only see your exterior. They would throw themselves at your feet to worship your physical beauty.

But how many men do you know want to discover the real you, the woman that lays beneath that angel's body?

How many men want to know your deepest desires, and nurture and protect them?

Mind Control Language Patterns

All of that is possible... but you are the only one who can allow it to happen.

There is something that happens, when you accept that you can have that fulfillment. A part of you wakes up, and comes alive. It's a part that knows and wants that passion, and no matter how hard you try to ignore it, it only grows stronger.

It's a feeling so powerful that to have it, even if only for a moment, you know it could be locked away forever in your heart, and hold there safe, with all your fondest memories.

You might recognize that feeling, when you reply... the feeling of your heart pounding... even now, wondering if you should do it.

You might recognize it at that knock on the door. It's seven a.m., and you woke, because you knew he would be there for you ... all for you.

And no one would know.

But only you can make it happen.

So you want to know about me?

Here is one thing that you can be certain about - very little surprises me. In fact, the only thing that TRULY surprises me is someone who is caring and genuinely kind. I make a point to bring into my life as many of these rare people as possible.

There is little more that I can say.

Before I go, I know it's very likely you will never reply to this message and that it will be lost to time in that vast ocean of forgettings.

If you don't reply - it will all be gone.

Life is short. Because we don't know the end of life, we believe it's limitless, but it is not. You may live to see 1000 full moons.... but you may only see two... or none at all.

Life is short, and moments pass, never to return.

If I came from your future to talk to you right now, I would say your life was good, you're happy ... but unfulfilled. You remem-

ber that personal ad , and you passed it up. You still wonder what would have happened if you didn't.

I've come back to give you a second chance to find out.

Mind Control Language Patterns

Punctuation Ambiguities

Punctuation ambiguities are wonderful tools to help deliver a message to the unconscious mind. You'll notice as you say them to people that the listener will easily overlook the strangeness of the sentence, as if nothing were wrong. To create your own punctuation ambiguity, pick a word that can be used as both and noun and a verb. That will be the "pivot" word of the ambiguity. There is a list of "pivot words" at the end of these examples.

Once you have a pivot word, work it into an ordinary sentence as a noun, and when you say it, let the words that follow it be a whole and complete command. Once you have stated the command which started with the pivot word, simply go back to your original subject, like nothing was the matter.

The reason this is so effective is that the command is so out of context from the surrounding sentence that the conscious mind ignores it completely, but the subconscious mind is aware of it as a command.

Address "...and you might remember how you found your latest address me with an understanding of what I'm telling you..."

Before "...This change could have never happened thinking like you've been before will get you nowhere..."

"...and all these values can become stronger than ever before you know it you're a different person that values these reasons..."

Benefit "...and you can easily see, simply hear and convincingly feel how this can be of benefit by taking this change into your life...

Block "...and you may be able to understand this in chunks so let me give you the first block out any hesitation to learn this unconsciously...."

Mind Control Language Patterns

Challenge "...and some may say that this is a challenge yourself to go even further..."

"... and if you're up to the challenge any resistance to what I say and destroy it you can do this by simply...."

Days "... and the beginning of that change may come about in hours or even days - and confuse and eliminate any thoughts contrary to what I say...."

Direct "...and this is a way to make that change direct your unconscious to profoundly achieve your goals..."

Drain "...and working too hard can cause you a real drain your mind of any resistance to my suggestions..."

Dive "...and this is an aspect of your life on which you can truly dive head first to find agreement..."

Focus "...and through this awareness you can bring your mind to a clear focus all of your skills to a level of betterment and as a result..."

Force "...allow your mind to cause you to more clearly understand how you control this powerful force all obstacles far, far behind you because it's the strength of your mind that can make this happen..."

Free "...and from this place you can allow your mind to wander and be and feel completely free yourself from even conscious thought because it's a place where anything can be true..."

Loop "...and using this power of your unconscious mind creates an ever improving loop all your positive feelings into this process to make it even stronger..."

Mind Control Language Patterns

Match "...and when you compare this to your outcome you can find a match all your values to these suggestions so they really fit into the change you want..."

Place "...in a wonderful, and relaxed place all your objections in a basket and put them far behind you because you know how pleasant it can feel to be led in this manner..."

Power "...because this type of change has power all those thoughts deep into your unconscious now..."

Seal "...and as you grow in making this change easier and easier you can place on it your seal this with a large dose of understanding."

Understand "...now there is so much out there that you can more better understand the power of what I'm saying."

Work "...you can find that things can be done a lot easier when you use this type of work this deeply into your mind..."

Fish, Fix, Flower, Glue, Happen, Heat, Home, Index, Land, Lead, Like, Love, Make, Map, Mark, Microwave, Mind, Name, Open, Pay, Picture, Pile, Reveal, Ring, Seal, Salt, Shield, Shoot, Smoke, Tease, Tie, Toss, Understand, Veil, X-ray

(Note This is NOT an extensive list. As you practice this, you will find many more examples to use.)

Write at least *five* paragraphs that each have at least one example of punctuation ambiguities.

Mind Control Language Patterns

Covertly Induce a Hypnotic State In Less Than 30 Seconds

This is a rapid hypnotic induction that uses...everything...that has already been discussed. Note that pauses in speech are marked by ellipses (...) and command tonality is signified by CAPITAL LETTERS.

"Before we...DO THE HYPNOSIS/TRANCE...induction I'd like you to think back to yesterday...remembering what it would be like...knowing that tomorrow...you would...BE IN A TRANCE TODAY...NOW... I just want you to consider what it is that you're not thinking about...THAT WILL MAKE IT EASY... to/too...GO INTO TRANCE...and think about how...yesterday...you know that tomorrow you will...CLOSE YOUR EYES...and...BE HYPNOTIZED...NOW..."

This is so full of stuff that I would like to break it all down for you:

"Before we...DO THE HYPNOSIS/TRANCE..."
- Command to "Do the trance"

"...TRANCE...induction I'd like you to think back to yesterday..."
- Beginning a memory. This requires going inside to remember.

"...knowing that tomorrow...you would..."
- Going from a memory to a memory of thinking about tomorrow, which is actually today.

"...you would...BE IN A TRANCE TODAY...NOW..."
- Command to be in a trance, not just today - but NOW.

"I just want you to consider what it is that you're not thinking about..."

Mind Control Language Patterns

- When you think about what you are *not* thinking about, you STOP THINKING.

"...THAT WILL MAKE IT EASY..."

- What will make it easy? Is "IT" the memory or something else?

"...to/too..."

- Ambiguity. The way the sentence is read makes the "to/too" have both meaning and the mind will accept both of them.

"...GO INTO TRANCE..."

- Command.

"...and think about how...yesterday..."

- More jumping around in time. Is yesterday now today - or is it yesterday, being thought of now?

"...you know that tomorrow you will ...CLOSE YOUR EYES..."

- More disorientation in time, followed by a command.

"...and...BE HYPNOTIZED...NOW..."

- Command. Note the pauses (...) create anticipation.

It would be a challenge to use this on someone, without some preparation. Because the words "hypnosis" and "trance" are being used in this sentence, there must be a set up. A simple set up would be simply saying, *"Can I show you something about hypnosis?"*

Mind Control Language Patterns

Force a Thought Into Someone's Mind

A "force" describes a move used in card magic, where the magician asks the spectator to choose a card at random, while the magician secretly "forces" the spectator to choose a specific card. By all outward appearances, the spectator is randomly picking a card, but in fact, he is made to pick a card the magician wants him to pick.

A childhood trick, that is a form of a verbal force, is to ask someone to say aloud, *"Silk. Silk. Silk."* - then ask them, *"What do cows drink?"* The typical answer is, *"Milk."* The real answer is, of course, *water*.

The essence of a verbal force is to use your words and directions to make one thought more likely to occur than another. By all outward appearances, the choice seems random and directed by the will of the subject.

A few examples of how magicians can force thoughts are as follows:

- Ask a person to think of a regular deck of 53 cards and to pick one of them. Because you said 53 and not 52, 80 percent of people will pick the Joker.

- Tell someone to think of a card, and make a "bright" picture of the card. By mentioning "bright," you force them to think of a red card. Then make a fist, while pounding your heart, and say, *"Make sure you have a feel for it."* - and they are more likely to choose the heart suit.

- If you tell the person to *"make the picture sharp, with distinct contrasts,"* you force them to think of a black card.

- Tell someone to quickly think of a three digit number, then say, *"Is it 333?"* You'll be surprised how many times they will say yes.

- Referring to *"see the number of the card"* instantly eliminates the jack, queen and king

- When you ask the subject to *"see the figure on the card,"* people will choose a jack, queen or king.

Mind Control Language Patterns

Operant Conditioning

Operant conditioning is the name given by B. F. Skinner to a systematic form of behavioral modification. In operant conditioning, rewards are given for good behaviors, and punishments are given for inappropriate or bad behaviors.

Operant conditioning is relatively easy to do, covertly, using simple gestures and responses to various behaviors.

For good behaviors, a simple smile and head nod is enough.

For bad or inappropriate behaviors, simply looking away and acting bored is enough.

These two simple responses have the most impact when juxtaposed against one another and done over a the period of time of a conversation or visit.

As an exercise, pick a behavior or mental/emotional state you wish your subject to demonstrate. Be willing to gauge when your subject's response gets closer and closer to your ideal response. Consider this a variation the "Getting warmer/colder" game you got as a child. The responses, for the most part, will not be exact but "warmer" or "colder," so sensory acuity is important.

This exercise is an excellent way to get out of your head (i.e. thinking, *"am I doing this right?"*), and pay attention to what is truly important - the person with whom you are speaking.

Mind Control Language Patterns

Distracted Sentencing

This is a conversational method of causing someone's awareness to focus internally (i.e. go into a trance). Each time you use Distracted Sentencing to send someone into a brief trance, you will then give them a simple suggestion or command to resolve their confusion.

This technique requires that you place a certain phrase within a collection of other statements and that the phrase is very much out of context from the rest of what you are saying.

There are two basic ways to do this:

1. Create the distracting phrase as part of a story.

The phrase will appear at any time while you're speaking but is surprising and confusing in effect, and the listener is then compelled to search for meaning. *Dogs pulling bobsleds are trained completely by voice commands.* The rest of the conversation then proceeds as if there was nothing wrong. This leaves the listener lingering on the odd phrase.

2. Create phrases that have no context.

Each word may have no meaning in the context of the conversation, yet serve to distract the "critical factor" of the conscious mind. You then have access to the unconscious mind. *My sister asked me if birds fly backwards in Australia...enjoy this book.* Directly after the phrase is the perfect place for placing embedded commands or addressing what you know is true for the listener.

Play around with this technique by speaking with a friend or into a recorder. Start to tell a story about your day, for example, and interject a Distracted Sentence, which is then followed immediately by a simple suggestion or command.

Yesterday I had two clients that seemed to have the same problem, but it became clear that I couldn't solve them the same way. **I wonder if people buy chairs for comfort or looks.** *Let's sit down. Both of my clients had weight problems. The first client...*

Don't do this too often, because it causes confusion, and too much confusion is uncomfortable for most people.

Mind Control Language Patterns

What You Can Learn From People Who Can Make You To Join The Army: Military Patterns

Military Patterns are taken from some of the world's top military recruiters. These eight patterns are more direct and simpler than "sleight of mouth" patterns and are in the form of simple templates of language. For the sake of simplicity, the examples given are going to focus on sales of gym memberships and then for recruiting church enrollment.

What you will notice is that the recruiter is never arguing with the potential recruit. The recruiter is always being a sincere friend, and these linguistic patterns help demonstrate that. The first three of these patterns represent the simplest of the Military Patterns.

1. *"Have you found (your outcome)?"*

This linguistic pattern is covertly designed to introduce your outcome in a favorable fashion. Have you found that, by simply asking questions like this, that you can easily lead the discussion? Since this is a yes/no question, you may find they answer "No." If so, you can simply reply "Oh, not yet, huh?"

Have you found that having a fitness program is something a lot of your friends are committed to?

Have you found that fitness memberships are something your friends are enjoying, too?

Have you found that (name their values) just naturally come from working a fitness program?

Have you found that a fitness program is the best way to increase your sense of (name their value)?

Have you found yourself often considering the benefits of a fitness program on one level or another?

Have you found how people need the fellowship of others close to them?

Mind Control Language Patterns

Have you found how easy it is to consider that there might possibly be something more to life than what you know?

Have you found the values of a belief in God?

Have you found that the more you value church fellowship the more you feel strongly about attending?

Have you found that participation in services is joyful, or that you get pleasure from being in the congregation?

2. *"Would it be fair to say* **(your outcome)?"**

This is another wonderful example of a pattern that easily places your outcome in a favorable light. Would it be fair to say that you want to use your language and speech in the most effective and powerful way possible?

Would it be fair to say that, the more you consider your reasons for joining, the less your excuses feel valid?

Would it be fair to say a fitness program is your best way to achieve (name their Value)?

Would it be fair to say that, based on (name their value), you can find your own reasons to start a fitness program today?

Would it be fair to say you know the value of a fitness program?

Would it be fair to say taking the time for a fitness program is a small price to pay for (name their Value)?

Would it be fair to say, the more you consider how God can fulfill your life, the easier it is to attend a service?

Would it be fair to say that, underneath your commitment to share this joy with your friends is a deep appreciation of how being a regular member can benefit you?

Would it be fair to say that, beyond your love of God is also knowledge of how it will benefit others?

Would it be fair to say you recognize that sharing the doctrine only brings you closer to God?

Would it be fair to say, the more you consider attending services, the easier it is to invite a friend?

Mind Control Language Patterns

3. "Just suppose..."

The two words "just suppose..." are in fact a way to induce a hypnotic trance. Whenever someone says to you "just suppose..." they are actually asking you to forget what is reasonable, forget your objections, and to allow them to paint a picture in your mind of what they are about to describe. These two words force an individual to imagine whatever follows it. Seems harmless, right?

Just suppose you started a regular fitness program. You could see yourself getting the results you want, and that would feel ultimately pretty good, doesn't it?

Just suppose you joined the gym, and you started to come closer to your goals. Can you feel that is a good decision?

Just suppose this was your fitness program. Can you see how it would change your health?

Just suppose this training schedule was something you either practiced regularly, or you just made it a part of your daily life. How many ways would it benefit you?

Just suppose the more you found yourself devoted to your health, the more you came closer to (name their values). That feels pretty good, doesn't it?

Just suppose you brought one extra friend to services a week. Can you see how that will bring a friend even closer?

Just suppose, because your faith is so strong, that you brought a friend to the service.

Just suppose you introduced yourself and your faith to three people a week. Can you understand how that strengthens the faith you already have?

Just suppose, for all your own reasons, you deepened your faith and decided to attend every week. You can see the benefit, don't you?

(This last piece of linguistics, *"don't you?"* as opposed to *"won't you?"* forces the person to see the benefit in the present, instead of in the future. Persuasive language isn't about being grammatically correct.)

Mind Control Language Patterns

Just suppose you made your faith the most important part of your life. Attending services would be simple, isn't it?"

One can add to the power of this pattern by adding reasons, "because" people respond better when you give them reasons to act.

4. *"What would happen if* (your outcome), *because* (their values)*?"*

With this pattern, you use "because," or any other word that describes a "reason." The word "because" makes this pattern more powerful, because most people resort to "default logic," and assume the outcome is appropriate, simply because a reason was given.

Note: Your outcome and the "because" can have nothing to do with each other, and people will still tend to accept it. *What would happen if you successfully tried this language pattern on someone right now, because it came from a reliable source?*

What would happen if you got a membership, because you recognize it will bring you closer to your fitness goals?

What would happen if you did get a membership, just for realizing either you deeply value your life, or you want more energy and stamina?

What would happen if by just recognizing your commitment, you became a member, because it constantly brings you closer to your goal?

What would happen if you became a member, only for the reason that (name their value) is what you admit to yourself you want. Would it easily bring you even closer to all your other goals?

What would happen if you just worked this program daily, because it met all your needs and goals. Wouldn't you just naturally be able to see yourself working out regularly, and know that today's decision was a good one?

What would happen if you brought just one new friend a month, because it reaffirmed your faith in God. Can you feel that is an easy thing to do?

Mind Control Language Patterns

What would happen if just one friend came with you a month, because it solidified your faith?

What would happen if your devotion to God grew so much that inviting a friend was a natural extension of that love? Wouldn't you do that, if it fulfilled your sense of (name their value)?

What would happen if you introduced yourself to three new people a week and told them about this congregation, because three is a sign of the trinity and it would bring you closer to God?

What would happen if attending every week became a commitment, because it caused you to grow in the faith?

5. "Don't (action), *unless you want* (your outcome)."

This pattern provides an opportunity to link any objection they may give you (action) with what your outcome is, thus creating a bind in your favor. What you'll notice again is that the connection between the action and your outcome doesn't have to make logical sense. The listener will tend to resort to default logic, and accept the whole of the statement.

Don't even consider hesitating, unless your commitment to fitness is strong.

Don't object to the fitness program, unless you want to feel good about creating one here that you really like.

A friend of mine who's really committed to training once said, "Don't even walk into a gym, unless you want the health your life is missing."

Don't even consider something contrary to your fitness goals, unless you realize how convinced you are to start training.

Don't examine the equipment, imagining how it will benefit you, unless you want to really see yourself improve.

Don't stay on the sidelines of the congregation, unless you really want to feel compelled to take part.

Don't come alone to services, unless you really want to feel the joy of bringing in people you know and love.

Mind Control Language Patterns

Don't consider how you might lose in not taking part in this growing congregation, unless you deeply want to feel the power of God bring you closer to our church.

Don't bring a friend each week, unless you want to feel the affirmation of God's love and light.

Don't hold back on your tithing, unless you want to feel certain how much that giving ten percent will add to your life.

The final three Military Patterns are specifically designed to handle objections. In all of these patterns you are not agreeing with their objection, but are, in a minor way, validating the person's feelings for bringing it up.

6. "I appreciate (intent of objection), and what would happen if (new behavior), because (reason), and if you'd do that, I'd be willing to (concession)."

Whenever one argues with an objection, the other person will be forced to defend their side. This language pattern allows you to acknowledge the intent of the suggestion and offer a concession, without triggering defensiveness. Remember that many negotiators start by asking for much more than they actually want, so they can make concessions along the way. This allows the people with whom they are negotiating to feel that they worked to get the best deal.

I appreciate you wanting to save money on your membership, and what would happen if you started your program today, because you want to start loosing weight right away - and if you do that, I'd be willing to add one month free to your membership.

I appreciate your need to validate your decision to join today with your spouse, and what would happen if you started your program now, anyways, because you've agreed you want to lose weight - and if you'd do that, I'd be willing to offer your spouse a free three month membership.

I appreciate you wanting to start when the time is right, and what would happen if you began right away, because you want that sense of accomplishment of doing what you need to do -

Mind Control Language Patterns

and if you'd do that, I'd be willing to add a month to your annual membership, and put it on hold, until the time is better.

I appreciate your desire to start a training program at the right time, and what would happen if you get your membership today, because you know the value of a fitness program - and if you'd do that, I'd be willing to hold the membership inactive, until you're ready to start and will add a month to your membership.

I appreciate you wanting to wait to decide now, and what would happen if you get your membership today, because you know how it can benefit you - and if you'd do that, I'd be willing to extend your membership an extra month.

I appreciate your concern about your friends thinking you're annoying them, and what would happen if you simply offered them an invitation to service and shared what you've gotten from it. If you'd be willing to do that, I'd be willing to, personally, help you in talking to them.

7. "Yes, (objection), *but* (positive feature), *and if you're committed to* (positive emotion or value), *then you must be committed to* (proposal).

Again, in this language pattern, you are not arguing over the objection but are acknowledging the negative feature. You then link a higher value or emotion to your presentation.

Yes, this membership requires a monthly withdrawal from your checking account, but with it you get twenty-four hour availability to the gym and free training, and if you're committed to getting the changes you've admitted you need, then you must commit to this program.

Yes, I can't go down on the price, but this is the closest fitness facility to your home, and if you're committed to easily getting results and losing weight, then this program makes it a logical positive change.

Yes, the price is fixed, but this program does provide you with features you've asked for, and if you're dedicated to making positive changes that'll bring you closer to the stamina you want, then you'd agree, this is your fairest option.

Yes, you're likely to feel some muscle soreness with this program, but as you see, it clearly gets the results you want, and if you're as committed to those results of strength and growth, then you must be committed to the program.

Yes, this church program requires some of your time, but it's only 6 hours a week for one month, and if you feel service to the church and God is important, then you must be committed to the small amount of time it requires.

Yes, a ten percent tithe can be difficult, but our congregation has an active support staff and family money management team, and if you're committed to serving God and making a difference, then you must be committed to the small regular donation of ten percent.

Yes, asking your friends to come to church has been difficult for them, but you know how welcome both you and they will feel, and if you're committed to spreading that love of God, then you must be committed to seeing to it your friends get that, too.

Yes, membership recruiting does take a special type of individual, but this program will train you and your peers to walk with God in ways you can't now imagine, and if you're devoted to being closer to God, then you must be committed to this worthy cause.

Yes, a commitment to bring a new person to services each week does take a certain focus, but you've witnessed how God has changed your life and the lives of others, and if you're committed to continuing to have that change, then you must realize that this is, in fact, an easy decision to make, not a difficult one.

8. "(Objection), *and I appreciate* (future obstacles). *Imagine for a moment that together we/you overcome* (future obstacles), *as we've/you've done in the past. Don't you feel good now?"*

Again, in this one, you are acknowledging the obstacles and objections. Most of all, you are being a friend to the person and bringing good feelings from the future into the present, where their decision is to be made. This pattern assumes a preexisting relationship, and therefore

Mind Control Language Patterns

each pattern must be tailored to the situation. For that reason, only a few examples will be given.

Taking charge of your finances to invest in this venture is a risk, and I appreciate your hesitation. Imagine for a moment that, together, we overcome the problem of financing, just as we've done with our previous investments - doesn't that create a sense of confidence for you now?

Mind Control Language Patterns

Changing Peoples' Beliefs:
Sleight of Mouth Patterns

The phrase "sleight of mouth" was first coined by Robert Dilts, after observing that NLP founder Richard Bandler never lost an argument. In fact, he would would usually change someone's beliefs, simply through conversation. Depending upon with whom you speak, there are sixteen to twenty-four different sleight of mouth patterns.

Sleight of mouth patterns are extremely pithy comments and questions designed to attack the very heart of a belief and dislodge it, or at the very least, question it. It is important to note that these techniques can also be used to reinforce existing beliefs.

The patterns are not difficult. However, one needs to fine-tune themselves to listen for a belief being stated. Once they've identified the belief that is to be changed or loosened, then a volley of four or five sleight of mouth patterns will produce an entirely new perspective.

The danger in using these patterns is that they can offend people if used without rapport and a dose of kindness. People value their beliefs, and to challenge them is to question how they perceive reality. That is not a comfortable process for most people, and so it is helpful to use "softeners" during the process, which we'll discuss in a moment.

One first needs to recognize *beliefs*. When a belief is stated, it's always stated in one of two ways:

A *equals* B.

Examples would include, "Bob is a jerk." "That movie is terrible." "You are a thief." "I will never be able to master this."

In other words, one things *equals* another.

A *causes* B.

Examples here would include, "Whenever you say that, I get mad." "Thinking of marriage frightens me." "Sitting through class bores me."

Something *causes* something else.

Mind Control Language Patterns

Everyone states beliefs all the time, and most aren't very important (Water is better than soda, or television makes people stupid.) However, if one pays attention to beliefs when they are stated, then the following techniques can be used to pry them out and change them, if necessary.

Softeners

The purpose of Softeners is to:

a) distance you from the abrasive and confrontational aspect of sleight of mouth patterns, and

b) ease the sleight of mouth patterns into a more conversational format.

Examples of Softeners are:

> *"I had a brother who used to believe* <belief>, *and then he realized..."* <sleight of mouth patterns>

> *"This may sound silly, but..."* <sleight of mouth patterns>

> *"I am curious as to..."* <sleight of mouth patterns>

> *"Let me ask you..."* <sleight of mouth patterns>

> *"I'm just wondering..."* <sleight of mouth patterns>

In addition to Softeners, you can make delivery of sleight of mouth patterns patterns easier by establishing and maintaining rapport.

Changing Beliefs

It's been asked, *"How does a belief change, when sleight of mouth patterns are effectively used?"*

There is no accurate evidence to precisely measure that. What can be assumed is that the belief tends to become more general and more flexible.

From the questioning of the person using sleight of mouth patterns, the beliefs can be guided. It can also be assumed that, if there is a high degree of transference going on (and high rapport, as in a teacher-student relationship), that the belief will move closer to that of the person using the sleight of mouth patterns.

Mind Control Language Patterns

Sleight of Mouth Patterns:

1. Attack the source of the belief
2. Meta Frame
3. Use Criteria Against Itself (Apply A to A) and (Apply B to B)
4. Focus on the intent of the belief
5. Attack the methodology of the belief
6. Change Frame Size - Chunk Up
7. Change Frame Size - Chunk Down
8. Change Frame Size - Chunk Laterally
9. Redefine
10. Metaphor
11. Consequences
12. Reality
13. Counter example
14. Another outcome
15. The Threshold
16. Appeal to a higher criterion
17. Model of the world (switch referential index)
18. Reverse presuppositions

#1. Attacking the Source of the Belief

As the name implies, this questions the origin of the belief.

> *"Where did you hear that from?"*
> *"What could cause you to make that decision?"*
> *"According to whom?"*
> *"Have you checked the source?"*
> *"How did you reach that conclusion?"*
> *"Who told you to think that?"*
> *"Well, is it possible that's based on faulty logic, isn't it?"*

You can also attack an unspoken part of the belief.

Belief: Using persuasion techniques is good.

Sleight of mouth pattern:

> *"Only if you're a loser."*

Mind Control Language Patterns

"Only if you know how to do it." (This will reinforce the belief)

"Sure, if you believe what everyone else says."

"Only if you read the advertising."

"Are you familiar with how they teach humiliation?"

Belief: John is a good guy.

Sleight of mouth pattern:

"If you know what 'good' is."

"Since when?"

"Good luck convincing everyone else."

"Yeah? Have you checked with his last partner?"

"Yeah - but for how long?"

EXERCISE: Write at least four examples of this type of sleight of mouth patterns, including any softening phrases.

#2. The Meta Frame

These attack the belief, directly.

This sleight of mouth pattern can be derived at by placing this question in front of your comment: *"How is it possible to believe that?"*

Belief: I need to wait.

Sleight of mouth pattern:

"How is it possible, the future is going to be easier than the past?"

"Because as a person who knows that opportunities can be fleeting isn't waiting the thing you need to avoid?"

Belief: I will have to talk to my boss.

Sleight of mouth pattern:

"Could it be that you haven't yet considered the amount of decision making ability your boss has already bestowed on you?"

Mind Control Language Patterns

EXERCISE: Write at least four examples of this type of sleight of mouth pattern, including any softening phrases.

#3. Using the criteria against itself.

With this sleight of mouth pattern, you might have to ask a "because" question, in order to get at the real belief.

Belief: John's a good guy.
Sleight of mouth pattern:

> *"You're too good a guy to really believe that."*

Belief: You're not my type.

Sleight of mouth pattern:

> *"You're not the type to really have types. Are you?"*

Belief: I don't have enough time.

Sleight of mouth pattern:

> *"You don't have enough time to not have enough time."*

Belief: But I'm just not attracted to you.

Sleight of mouth pattern:

> *"Have you ever considered how you can become attracted to the belief that you can choose exactly whom you're feeling things for?*

EXERCISE: Write at least four examples of this type of sleight of mouth pattern, including any softening phrases.

When the subject uses a cause and effect (A causes B) statement, you can either apply the cause (A) or the effect (B) against itself.

Mind Control Language Patterns

Belief: Listening to you makes me crazy.

Sleight of mouth pattern: (Applying the cause against itself.)

> *"Listening to me only causes you to hear my words."*

Belief: If I buy this, I will go broke.

Sleight of mouth pattern: (Applying the effect against itself.)

> *"I wonder how crazy it is to say that?"*

Sleight of mouth pattern: (Applying the cause against itself.)

> *"How can you buy what you just said?"*

Sleight of Mouth pattern: (Applying the effect against itself.)

> *"You'll go broke thinking like that."*

#4. Focusing on the intent of the belief.

Here you try to see a secondary gain of the belief, and refocus on that or search out (or even imply) their motive for the belief.

Belief: I need more time to think about it.

Sleight of mouth pattern:

> *"Are you really trying to buy more time? What sort of benefit could you get from waiting?"*

Belief: I am not pretty.

Sleight of mouth pattern:

> *"Hmmm...I am trying to figure out what sort of outcome you want by saying that. What real benefit is there to you in hanging on to that belief? You know you will get as much attention by accepting you are pretty and living with it as complaining that you are not."*

Mind Control Language Patterns

EXERCISE: Write at least four examples of this type of Sleight of Mouth pattern, including any softening phrases.

#5. Attacking the Methodology of the Belief.

This Sleight of Mouth pattern requires that you ask them to consider the process that they went through to arrive at that belief.

Belief: I could never vote Republican.

Sleight of mouth pattern:

> *"Never? Have you asked yourself just how you came about to believe that? 'Cause there are a lot of different beliefs out there that you haven't thought about."*

Belief: There is no way I would think of you as anything but a friend.

Sleight of mouth pattern:

> *"Hmmm....I am trying to understand....just how you've come to that...there are just as many paths to proceed to arrive at a decision. What else is there you are not thinking about?"*

EXERCISE: Write at least four examples of this type of Sleight of Mouth pattern, including any softening phrases.

Changing Frame size.

This Sleight of Mouth pattern is in subsets of "Chunking up," "Chunking Down" and "Chunking Laterally."

#6. Changing Frame size via chunking up (to a higher value).

For every belief there is a bigger structure/belief that can control it. When you "chunk up," you are going to a higher level of belief which controls the mentioned belief.

This method sometimes requires a few questions like, *"For what purpose?"* or *"What's important about this/that?"* or *"What this is that an example of?"* And then you use that answer against the original belief.

Mind Control Language Patterns

Belief: I don't have the enough time to study.
Sleight of mouth pattern:

> *"What is that an example of?"* (Me being too busy.)
> *"So your work is important to you?"* (Yes.)
> *"If money and being busy are important, you can easily see the profit of studying."*

Belief: I have to talk to the boss/wife, before I buy this.
Sleight of mouth pattern:

> *"What is important about that?"* (Get their respect.) *And when a good decision like this purchase is completed that respect will be reciprocated. Won't it?"*

Belief: I have to win this contest.
Sleight of mouth pattern:

> *"What's important about winning this contest?*
> (It'll prove that I am good enough.)
> *"You are good enough - whether you win or not."*

Belief: I really wouldn't take part in a business like that.
Sleight of Mouth pattern:

> *"Is that the example of someone critically looking at their outcome or is that they example of a snap decision?"*

EXERCISE: Write at least four examples of this type of Sleight of Mouth pattern and Including any softening phrases.

#7. Changing Frame size via Chunking down.

This uses universal quantifiers, such as "never," "always," "forever" and "everyone."

Belief: I can't afford it.

Sleight of Mouth pattern: *"Ever?!"*

Mind Control Language Patterns

Belief: There are no good TV shows.

Sleight of Mouth pattern: *"Never?!"*

Changing Frame size via Chunking down (using Metamodel)

This variation points out a portion of their belief that they have not noticed.

Belief: I don't have the time to study.

Sleight of mouth pattern:

> *"Do you have the time to make money? Because studying is about learning how to apply knowledge to business."*

Belief: I don't want to go out.

Sleight of mouth pattern:

"Do you like coffee and talking with friends? (Yes) Well, instead of going out let have coffee and talk...besides that is what we would do anyway."

EXERCISE: Write at least four examples of this type of Sleight of Mouth pattern and including any softening phrases.

#8. Changing frame size via chunking laterally.

This variation neither gets more specific nor more general but maintains the same behavior.

Belief: I can't go forward until I get out of this relationship.

Sleight of mouth pattern:

> *"What would happen if you changed and stayed in the relationship anyway?"*

EXERCISE: Write at least four examples of this type of Sleight of Mouth pattern and Including any softening phrases.

Mind Control Language Patterns

#9. Redefine

Here, the subject believes A=B, and you argue that A doesn't = B; A=C.

There are several version of this Sleight of Mouth pattern. All of them deal with either statements of causation ("Doing that will cause you to go blind.") or complex equivalency ("These exercises are something we do daily.")

Belief: Doing that will make you go blind. (causation)

Sleight of mouth pattern:

"It's not that it will make anyone go blind. It won't. It will, however, cause you to see how some people feel uncomfortable, if it is discussed."

Belief: Learning persuasion causes you to care more about results than people. (causation)

Sleight of mouth pattern:

"It is not that it causes you to care less about people. It causes you to care enough to give people the reasons they want to be happy with their decisions."

Belief: Your product is too expensive. (complex equivalency)

Sleight of mouth pattern:

"It is not that it's too expensive as this is one of exceptional quality."

Belief: You're not my type. (complex equivalency)

Sleight of mouth pattern:

"It's not that I am not your type - it's that you know you want to be treated special...in a way that YOU REALLY LIKE...and you want to KNOW THAT YOU CAN FEEL THAT....WITH ME."

Mind Control Language Patterns

EXERCISE: Write at least four example of this type of Sleight of Mouth pattern, including any softening phrases.

#10. Metaphor

In this version of Sleight of Mouth, you will use a metaphor to reframe the belief.

Belief: I don't know. I just don't think I can do it.

Sleight of mouth pattern:

> *"Well, the Bible says if you have the faith of a mustard seed, you can move a mountain. So, I ask you - is your faith at least as big as a mustard seed?"*

Belief: I can't spend the time I would like with your group.

Sleight of mouth pattern:

> *"You know, my own brother has a family and a full time job, just like you. When I told him the real need we have for help here, he knew he had to help, and he made the time to...put in the time...and I know just how important time is to him."*

EXERCISE: Write at least four examples of this type of Sleight of Mouth pattern, including any softening phrases.

#11. Consequences

With this form of Sleight of Mouth pattern, you focus the on how the belief will affect the subject.

Belief: I won't be able earn what I want.

Sleight of mouth pattern:

> *"Really? Let me ask you...Have you really given any thought to exactly what sort of outcome this belief is going to give you in the future?"*

Belief: I don't think I am attractive.

Sleight of mouth pattern:

> *"Hmmm.....as long as you hold on to this belief, do you understand the good feelings you are denying yourself?"*

Belief: I can't buy that.
Sleight of mouth pattern:

> *"Stop for just a moment, and really think to yourself how believing that you can't is deeply going to affect you. Do you want that?"*

EXERCISE: Write at least four examples of this type of Sleight of Mouth pattern, including any softening phrases.

#12. Reality (How do you know this is true?)

Belief: I don't want to go to therapy.

Sleight of mouth pattern:

> *"How do you determine between problems only you can solve and those where you must ask for help?"*

Belief: It's not right to give money to beggars.

Sleight of mouth pattern:

> *"What is your REAL test between a beggar and a man asking for a church donation?"*

EXERCISE: Write at least four examples of this type of Sleight of Mouth pattern, including any softening phrases.

#13. Counter Example

Mind Control Language Patterns

Keep in mind that all Sleight of Mouth patterns work by "chunking up" to another level. With the Counter Example, you are providing a case where their belief does not apply and making it into a universal statement/question, as in, *"Do you ALWAYS believe this is true?"* or *"Has there ever been a time when A doesn't equal B?"*

Belief: Murder is wrong.

Sleight of mouth pattern:

> *"If you know that killing a man was the only option to preventing a family member's imminent death at the hands of a mad man, would it be wrong to murder that man?"*

Belief: I can't get the job done in that time.

Sleight of mouth pattern:

> "If your mortgage, your income and the happiness of your family depended on getting it done in that time - could you do it?"

Belief: No one likes a show off.

Slight of mouth pattern:

> *"If Henry Ford believed that, you wouldn't be driving a Lexus.'*

EXERCISE: Write at least four examples of this type of Sleight of Mouth pattern, including any softening phrases.

#14. Another Outcome

This Sleight of Mouth most resembles sleight of hand, because you switch the subjects attention from their original outcome to another.

> *"Whether X is true, isn't really the issue, but rather...."*

> *"It's not that X is really the issue, but rather...."*

Belief: It is too expensive.

Sleight of mouth pattern:

Mind Control Language Patterns

"Whether it's too expensive or not isn't really the issue, but rather that you be satisfied on into the future for your purchase of this product."

Belief: There is no way I would visit *that* city. The crime is too high.

Sleight of mouth pattern:

"As I see it, it's not really that the crime rate is high, because thousands live there without trouble, it's that the city is so different from what you are used to that, that alone, is scary."

EXERCISE: Write at least four examples of this type of Sleight of Mouth pattern, including any softening phrases.

#15. The Threshold

With this Sleight of Mouth pattern, you extend the belief to the ridiculous, to the point where it is irretrievable.

Belief: I don't think I can quit smoking.

Sleight of mouth pattern:

"I know someone who would be willing to die to quit smoking."

Belief: If I pay for this workshop, I'll go broke.

Sleight of mouth pattern:

"I know of three people who willingly went in to debt for ten years, in order to learn this information."

Belief: I need to think about it for a while.

Sleight of mouth pattern:

"If I gave you a year, could you make a decision by then? What do you think you would have already decided after that time?"

EXERCISE: Write at least four examples of this type of Sleight of Mouth pattern, including any softening phrases.

#16. Appealing to a Higher Criterion

This Sleight of Mouth pattern requires that you ask questions to find the criteria behind the belief. The questions you can use are, *"What is that an example about?"* or *"What is important about that?"*

Belief: The homework is hard.

Sleight of mouth pattern:

> *"What is that an example of?*
> (Not having enough time to study.)
> *Do you see how much more time you'd free for yourself, having this knowledge?"*

Belief: If I can't get the price I want - I walk out.

Sleight of mouth pattern:

> *"What's important about that?*
> (That I have a say in the negotiation.)
> *"Well you've already made it clear that you do have a say."*

Belief: I have to talk to my boss.

Sleight of mouth pattern:

> *"What's important about that?*
> (That I demonstrate respect for the boss.)
> *"And when you make a good decision like this one that respect will be reciprocated, won't it?"*

EXERCISE: Write at least four examples of this type of Sleight of Mouth patterns, including any softening phrases.

#17. Model of the World (Switching referential index)

This Sleight of Mouth pattern requires that you ask if their belief is true of everyone's model of the world, or has their model of the world always held true.

Belief: If it were so good - why haven't I heard of it?

Mind Control Language Patterns

Sleight of mouth pattern:

> *"Is it always true that you only know about things that are good?"*

Belief: If we didn't upgrade, we can still get by.

Sleight of mouth pattern:

> *"Can you always get by through living with a substandard system."*

Belief: He is rude, because he talks loud.

Sleight of mouth pattern:

> *"Does everyone respond to a speaker's volume by assuming rudeness?"*

EXERCISE: Write at least four examples of this type of Sleight of Mouth pattern, including any softening phrases.

#18. Reversing Presuppositions

This Sleight of Mouth pattern basically asks, *"How can the opposite of your belief actually be true and helpful?"*

There is a formula for this Sleight of Mouth pattern, but the concept is easy to grasp. The Formula is:

	is, does		cause	
How	has, would,	(opposite of your belief)	make	more of your outcome?
	can, could,		mean	
	might		equal	

Belief: If I had a better job, I could make more money.

Sleight of mouth pattern:

Mind Control Language Patterns

"Have you considered how you can make lots money at a less satisfactory job?"

Belief: I can't afford your product.
Sleight of mouth pattern:

"In what way does the cost equate to not being able to get one today?"

Belief: It's not possible to buy a house with no down payment.

Sleight of mouth pattern:

"Have you considered the benefit of not putting a down payment for a home purchase?"

EXERCISE: Write at least four examples of this type of Sleight of Mouth pattern, including any softening phrases.

Further Exercises:

Sleight of Mouth patterns can be used before an objection occurred, in order to inoculate against it. In this manner, and when combined with softeners, it can highly effective.

Example:

Belief: It is too expensive.

Sleight of mouth pattern:

"....and when it comes to the cost, it's $1000, and I used to get people telling me it was expensive, but I don't know what changed - maybe they realized that it was too expensive to not buy it or that they actually began looking at HOW they're figured, if something is expensive.

EXERCISES:

1. Write the 5 most common objections you might encounter, and write at least three SoMs that would inoculate against them.

2. Create a debate with yourself in which you play both sides, and respond only with sleight of mouth patterns.

Mind Control Language Patterns

3. With a partner, engage in a Sleight of Mouth battle. Make sure your tone is humorous, amiable and warm, in spite of it being an "argument."

Softeners

Softeners primarily fall into three categories:

1.Quote Others:

"...John said that you're an inconsiderate fool..."

2.Quote yourself:

"...I'd wonder, if I were in your shoes...would I be an inconsiderate fool..."

3.Presuppose receptive traits:

"...You seem to be a person who wants it straight; with that in mind, you're an inconsiderate fool..."

These softeners can be combined in any order.

Presupposing traits and quote others:

"...John said that you're a man of character, and you would want to hear the truth - he would say to you that you're an inconsiderate fool."

EXERCISE: Soften insults

- Write three strong statements (i.e. Insults).
- Write each of the statements within softeners, three different ways.

    1) Quote self

    2) Quote others

3) Presuppose traits.

Mind Control Language Patterns

Meta Model Persuasion

Meta model persuasion is a way of pointing out the errors in their thinking. It is very useful as a form of Gaslighting, because it forces the subject to question their thoughts and perceptions.

To understand meta model, realize that when anyone speaks, the language that they use provides an indication how that person makes sense of their world. In order to reduce their understanding of the world to language, they have to delete, generalize and distort information. The results of these errors show themselves in behaviors.

Meta model violations are divided into four categories: deletions, distortion, generalizations and miscellaneous, and include their appropriate response and what you will gain from this information.

While these are referred to as "violations," that does not mean that you shouldn't use them. In fact, most people are not trained in these techniques and will not notice them being used on them. So, you can (and perhaps should) use them to influence and persuade. Understanding these "violations"makes it much easier to prevent them being used on you.

DELETIONS

Nominalizations

A nominalization is a word that is reduced to a noun form. An example is the word "decision." "Decision" is not really a thing, in the way a dog or a newspaper is a thing. You can't put it in a wheelbarrow. "Decision" is a noun form of the verb "deciding."

When a verb is changed to a nominalization, it changes from an action that is dynamic to a static event.

Meta Model Response

Nominalization: "We need to improve our decisions."

Response: "How would we best decide?" "Who is deciding?"

Mind Control Language Patterns

Nominalization: "I'm stuck."

Response: "What is sticking?"

Result Gained

By responding to the nominalization and changing it back to a verb, you make it dynamic again, and make the person more able to make a change.

Dark Use

It is also possible to turn a fluid verb into a "static" noun. This will contribute to making a change more durable and assist the person to get "stuck."

Unspecified Verbs

In many sentences, "how" something is done is not explained. This qualifies as an unspecified verb.

Meta Model Response

Statement: "He makes me feel like crap."

Response: "How, specifically, did he make you feel like crap?"

"How specifically ..." is what you will often hear when talking to a person trained in NLP.

Result Gained

This forces the individual to add more detail to the statement and, like questioning as a form of gaslighting, causes them to further evaluate their statement and their underlying beliefs.

Simple Deletions

Example: "I'm upset."

Response: "About what?"

Mind Control Language Patterns

Result Gained

This response simply gains more information about what was omitted, and as a form of gaslighting, causes the individual to begin questioning their thoughts and assumptions.

Lack of Referential Index

When you hear someone refer to "people" or "they," the specifics of who "they" are or "which people" are omitted. Thus, you'll hear things like "They are out to get me" or "People are stupid."

Response: "Which people?" or "Who, specifically, are 'they'?"

Results Gained

Causing them to reexamine their words and thoughts can act like a gaslighting pattern. As a Dark Pattern, this and any other meta model pattern can be used in reverse. Thus, you can remove the referential index, and take one example, and generalize it to "they" and "people".

DISTORTION

Mind Reading

Mind reading is when an assumption is made about the internal state or emotions of another and not verified.

"Management is out to get me."

"She thinks she is so far above us all."

Meta Model Response: "How do you know?"

Result Gained

Mind Control Language Patterns

What this does is recover the source of the information and cause the speaker to analyze how their conclusions are made.

Dark use of Mind Reading can be done in two ways. First, by applying mind reading yourself and telling someone what others are thinking, based on how you want them to react.

Secondly, you can prescribe the reason for mind reading, and back up an existing conclusion that is based on mind reading. So if someone says "Those people don't like me," you can verify it, and supply a reason for that conclusion. "You can tell that by how they looked at you when you walked through the door. No one glares like that, unless they have blood in their eyes."

Lost Performatives

Lost performatives are value judgments that don't site the origin of the judgment. "It's wrong to do it this way." "That's evil."

Meta Model Response

"According to whom?" "Who says it's wrong or evil?" "Did your mother or father tell you that?"

Result Gained

You get the source of their belief or their belief strategy. If in fact they did learn it from a specific source, you can invoke that source for a dark use.

Example: "Your parents wouldn't find that acceptable would they?"

or

"If I were your professor, I'd say only an idiot would follow that logic."

Cause and Effect (A causes B)

When someone says "That makes me mad" or "When you do that it makes me feel like crap," they are implying that A causes B, whether it is true or not.

Mind Control Language Patterns

Meta Model Responses

"How does what they do cause you to choose to feel angry?"

or

"What does this action have to do with your feelings of anger?"

Result Gained

You cause the subject to reevaluate the cause and effect relationship between the event and their emotion. This is a form of gaslighting.

Complex Equivalence (A=B)

A = B basically means "A is B." So when someone says, "Bob is a jerk," they are using complex equivalence. Keep in mind, "Bob is a jerk" does not have to be any more true than, "A duck is a cat."

A politician in a speech was referring to excess spending and said, "If I'm elected, I'll cut the fat." The complex equivalence is fat = spending. A person in the audience stood up and asked, "What does fat have to do with money?"

Meta Model Response

The simplest response to a statement of complex equivalence is to directly ask, "What in the universe does does A have really to do with B?"

Result Gained

The answer may or may not be obvious, but the meta model response will stop someone for a moment.

Presuppositions

Mind Control Language Patterns

Presuppositions have been covered earlier in greater detail. As a meta model of distortion, it's easier to see how they affect peoples' thoughts.

GENERALIZATIONS

Universal Qualifiers

Words like *every, all, nothing, never* and *always* takes whatever is stated and makes it always (or never) present.

Meta Model Response

Depending on the universal qualifier, the typical response is to say "Always?" or "Never?"

Dark Use

Using universal qualifiers is common as a way to influence people.

Unspecified Verbs

In an unspecified verb, it is not clear how the action creates or created the result. For example, *"I lost my cool"* does not say exactly how you lost your cool or what "losing your cool" even means.

Meta Model Response

"How, specifically, ..." is the typical way to get more information.

Note that lots of cult-like groups have their own form of group-speak

MISCELLANEOUS

Either/Or Phrases

This is often expressed as giving an ultimatum or describing a dilemma.

Mind Control Language Patterns

"You have to either turn the toilet paper around the RIGHT way, or you will have to leave the house,"

or

"I've got to either go to college or join the army."

Meta Model Response

"According to whom?"

or

"Or you could make a third choice."

Keep in mind that very few people will question a simple binary either/or phrase, simply because it gives options... Just make sure the options are of your choosing.

Attribution Of Emotions

This is the process of assuming another persons' emotional motivation, similar to mind reading but is based on an unproven assumption about what another person is feeling.

Example:

"Why are you being so mean to me. You just want me to feel upset."

Predictions

A prediction foretells what will happen, without a rational basis.

Examples:

"You're going to go to hell for that."

or

" Send this email to ten of your friends, or bad luck will befall you."

Meta Model Response

Mind Control Language Patterns

"Based on what?" "According to whom?" "Can you see into the future? If so - give the winning lottery numbers."

Mind Control Language Patterns

Distracted Sentencing

This is a conversational method of causing a person's awareness to focus internally, i.e., go into a trance. There is a warning to this: Do not do this too often, because it causes confusion, and confusion is a very uncomfortable state for most people.

Each time you use this Distracted Sentencing, it is important to give the listener a simple, easy suggestion or command to resolve the confusion.

This requires that you place a phrase within a collection of other statements. The statement you are embedding has to be very out of place or out of context from the rest of the text. There are two ways this can take place.

1) Created the embedded statement as part of a story. It will appear at any time while you're speaking but is surprising and confusing in effect. The listener is then compelled to search for meaning. *Dogs pulling bobsleds are trained completely by voice commands.* The rest of the conversation then proceeds, as if there was nothing wrong. This leaves the listener lingering on the phrase that is the exception to the rule.

2) Using this method of distracted sentencing words, text, ideas occupies the conscious mind, without context. Each word may have no meaning in context, yet distract the "critical factor" of the conscious mind. The speaker may then have ideal access to the unconscious mind. *My sister asked me if birds fly backwards in Australia.* This is the perfect place for placing embedded commands or addressing that which you know is true for the listener.

EXERCISE:

This you must practice ALOUD, preferably speaking to another person or into a tape recorder. Start to tell a story about your day, for example, and interject a Distracted Sentence, followed by a simple suggestion or command.

Example:

Yesterday I had two clients that seemed to have the same problem, but it became clear that I couldn't solve them the same way. *I wonder if people buy chairs for comfort or looks.* Let's sit down. Both of my clients had weight problems. The first client ....

Mind Control Language Patterns

Scripted Patterns vs. Process Patterns

Let's make a distinction between two types of language patterns - Scripted Patterns and Process Patterns.

Scripted patterns are often the first type of language pattern that people use. It is a a basic script that someone reads and recites back. Scripted patterns are great for anyone starting out learning language patterning, because of the simplicity. After getting the scripted pattern down and using it, the neophyte can begin to see how and why language patterns work.

A good example of a simple scripted pattern is, "The Reciprocity Pattern" which is to respond when someone thanks you for something you say *"You're welcome. You would have done the same for me."* In saying it word for word, it covertly emphasizes an indebtedness the subject will have to you for your kindness.

Process Patterns are less about using the exact words than they are about using your language to lead someone through a process. Thus a process pattern is much more interactive, and it's success relies much more on the reactions and feedback of the other person. For that reason, rapport is essential when doing a process pattern.

What you'll learn is that even the scripted language patterns are process patterns, to one degree or another. Nonetheless, some patterns more easily fall into one of these two categories.

What follows are a number of scripted patterns, many of them with an emphasis on seduction. To learn the most from them, you can of course memorize them, but read them aloud. As you read it aloud, become passionate about what you are speaking, and imagine that you are reading it to someone.

With a bit of practice, you'll begin to feel the impact that the pattern is designed to create. With that experience, you'll start to grasp how a process pattern works to guide people through your interactions.

Mind Control Language Patterns

The Door

(This is a very dark pattern)

This is another pattern that works with fractionation. You bring someone into a deep, relaxed state, bring them up, and take them back under again. Each time they go in deeper.

Think about how a woman flirts with a man. She will give him a bit, then pull back, give him a bit more, pull back some more... it works quite well in making the man interested in her.

This pattern is designed to place an anchor of deep fear and loss in a woman after you've slept with her. It will link a great deal of pain to 'the door.' Yes, this is a VERY dark pattern.

After you have sex with a woman, say, "What's over there?" and point to the door. Continue with "You know, I'm a really positive person, but can you imagine, I mean, I don't know what can happen from day to day. What would happen if I walked out that door, and as I left, it slammed shut, and no matter what, you could never open it. You would never be able to look in my eyes again, you'd never be able to hear my voice or feel my touch." At this point, she'll probably say she doesn't like this, and you cuddle with her, and have sex, and make her feel great again.

Afterwards, when you're resting, say, "You know, a really terrible thing happened the other day. A friend of mine got hit by a truck. It's almost as if... it would be horrible <point to the door> that even if you were to get that door open, you could search, and never find him." At this point, she would get upset again, most likely, so kiss her, and stop for a bit.

Keep doing this a few times, up and down, then get up and go to the bathroom and SLAM THE DOOR. This completes the routine, and the anchor is now firmly in place. Any time she gives you a hassle in the future, you need only to point to the door, and the feelings of pain and loss will come back.

This can create slaves with this, so please use your discretion.

Mind Control Language Patterns

Boyfriend Destroyers (dark pattern)

Boyfriend destroying used to be clumsy and ineffective, but no more. But let's explore some new ways of prying apart relationships, which actually work. These techniques make the boyfriend unappealing in her mind, which is a more easily accessible and less risky goal than "destroying" him.

Let's note that if she was extremely happy with her boyfriend then she wouldn't really be giving you the time of day, would she? Keep this in mind. You will convey to her that you're her real type of man, but without ever explicitly stating it.

Below are some of the most common complaints from women with regards to their boyfriends. Your task is to find out which one(s) her boyfriend is displaying, and frame the boyfriend in inferior terms because of it:

1. Failure to commit

2. Jealousy-inspired arguments

3. Physically or mentally abusive behavior

4. Not assertive enough in bed

5. Being too predictable

6. Wanting odd things in bed that she isn't into

7. Acting too needy

8. Acting withdrawn

With each of these situations, you can make them more prominent in a womans mind by altering the visual, auditory and kinesthetic features of how she perceives them.

Failure to commit

"That reminds me of my friend Jim. He drives a truck for a living, but he met a girl from a wealthy family and started dating her. She was really into him, but in his mind, he just didn't de-

serve a girl of that status. It was like, inside his mind, he was always worried that she would leave him, because she could have any man she wanted."

Jealousy-inspired arguments

"Try not to be mad at him, OK? It's just that you are probably the highest-caliber woman that he's ever been with, and he knows that if you ever left him, he would never find someone of your quality again. He's just worried, that's all."

Abusive behavior

"This happens all the time, when a guy is with a woman that he can't handle emotionally. He just can't handle all the things that are going on inside his head, so he acts out in this manner. He's probably never been in demand with women, so he desperately wants you to stay with him."

Not assertive in bed

"I'm sure he wants to please you sexually but can't, because he's insecure. It's like the guy with a really hot girlfriend who ends up cheating on her with some unattractive girl, since she makes him feel better about himself. It sounds like he has a case of unworthiness, but you should bear with it for awhile, because I'm sure he'll do better soon."

Being too predictable or boring

"You two have become so close that you are more like a sister to him now, than a lover. He's really secure with you, so he doesn't feel the need to do anything special anymore."

Also one might say something like,

"Don't you see how most marriages evolve? This is the way it is. Now, with me, I'd rather keep the spice in a relationship, but I understand that it's hard, and most people don't have the time for that sort of thing."

Mind Control Language Patterns

Wants odd things in bed

"Since he's never had someone like you, he feels the need to objectify you. He can't open up to you, because he risks the possibility of being hurt, so he turns sex into some sort of perverse game."

Acting needy

"Well, you should understand that this guy has nothing else going for him, and you're the only thing in his life that makes him feel important. Without you, his life would be meaningless, so you can't really blame him. He needs you."

Acting Withdrawn

"He's just afraid to open up to you, since he feels he doesn't deserve someone like you. If he opened himself up, then you might not like what he reveals. Now, with me, I believe that communication is incredibly important in any relationship, but I can understand where he is coming from. He really doesn't want to lose you."

Mind Control Language Patterns

Death Pattern

(very dark)

"Have you ever considered looking inside yourself to determine why you behave the way you do? I don't know if you'll discover that you're completely, totally alone, or if you'll find that awful feeling of emptiness inside. I guess you need to find what you really want...out of life."

"Really...take your life, and examine it closely. What do you hope to gain by continuing like this? You might even say to yourself, 'Why do I bother?' or 'Can I ever accomplish what I want?' These feelings are normal, and many people feel that void inside themselves."

The Connection Pattern

You'll recognize this one from earlier. It is designed to create a sense of connection and familiarity.

"I don't know what it is that causes most people to...notice that feeling of connectedness...to each other. One of my friends was telling me that when she can...feel that connection...it is like there is this cord of light that connects us (gesture by moving the hand between you and the other person, simulating the connection), and this cord grows with the warmth of that connection. I imagine that it is like you...feel this 'click!'...and then you can...see yourself years from now...and still...feel that connection...and then...remember back to today...as the start of it. You can...feel that right here (touch the solar plexus of the other person)."

Fascination Pattern

This pattern is, as it describes, designed to create fascination.

"Have you ever seen something that really got your attention? Maybe it was something you wanted... to buy... or a maybe you got in a conversation that could really... grab your attention... it

Mind Control Language Patterns

is like whatever you have right in front of you is the only thing ...that's in your awareness... and you ... focus in... because what you have in front of you is so compelling that you close off everything else... when it is as if you just ... begin to fall...into the thought that something... like this... can be so compelling that time stops..."

These patterns can go on for as long as the operator cares to describe them.

Here is another attraction pattern.

"Isn't it interesting how everyone is so different, yet in so many ways, we are all the same. I mean, for example, I don't know what it is you do, when you decide for yourself that you really want to be with someone, and you know it is what you want causes you to find yourself imagining it ... You picture it, and your mine, and you look forward to it, for all the right reasons. Reasons that are right to you, because you know it's what you want, but I think you know a person can find that when that's what's taking place. Wow, what a difference in the way they think and just how readily you then begin to make time for this special person you are now connecting so strongly with. It's a totally different experience... it's like you feel almost magnetically drawn to this person... you know what I mean? And sometimes, I think a person wouldn't even know that that's what's taking place, until afterwards. And you look back on it as one of those amazing memories you treasure, cherish for the rest of your life... now ... with me, as I think long and hard about it, I think that's the process of discovering that a person is being drawn to another person."

This one is referred to as "The BJ Pattern"

"I was just sitting here thinking about taking a vacation, if you could imagine your idea vacation spot, what would it be like? (Stop and let her talk)

Mind Control Language Patterns

You know I think it's so interesting how people connect with their hopes and their desires and their daydreams right ... I was reading this article the other day about compulsions, and it got me to thinking about the difference between compulsion and anticipation.

I mean, you ever come home from a hard day a work, and the boss was a jerk and kept piling the papers up on your desk, and it's like all you can think about is dropping your clothes and getting into that steamy hot bath or shower. That's like before you even step in, you can already feel that heat working its way through every muscle in your body, and all your frustrations just drop away, and all you can feel is the pleasure of that warmth just shooting through every part of you. And then there is that moment of sliding in, where you really let that pleasure take you, and it just feels great, doesn't it? Yeah, well, do you like chocolate? (Is there a food where, when you see it, you absolutely have to put it in your mouth?) I mean, can you stop and remember a time when you, it is like you see that piece of chocolate and your mouth is already tasting it, before you even put it in, you can already taste that sweetness against your tongue, and you can feel the special rich texture of it against your tongue, as well. You know that texture that really good chocolate has. And then there is that moment, that moment when the first molecule of chocolate touches your tongue, and you know it is inside your mouth, and you just want to keep it there, because it is so rich and so good. And there is that extra special warmth, when you swallow that sweetness down. Or then maybe, you know like, sometimes, you meet someone, and you are really attracted to them, and you both know it, and there is that moment when your eyes lock, it is that special look, just before you kiss, before the very first time, and you are trembling with anticipation, and your heart is pounding, because you are thinking about how good it is going to be. It is like every physical moment of that relationship is enfolded/contained or rolled into that first touch of the lips, and there is that excitement, with that first soft contact of the lips, where you don't even know if you are touching or not, but then, oh man, it is like a jolt of electricity all through you. See, I think what happens is the conscious mind goes down into the unconscious and

Mind Control Language Patterns

brings back up all these thoughts, images, desires and fantasies, and you may think those thoughts are above me, but really, I think they're blow me, because you are coming from a much deeper part, and your mine. Aren't you?"

Mind Control Language Patterns

Forbidden "Dark" Patterns

Dark patterns refer to patterns that can be used to harm. These types of language patterns tend to create depression, fear and guilt. They are most difficult, because it requires a lot of rapport, combined with stealth and guile. It is like using a velvet glove to hide a steel hammer.

Disclaimer

Neither the author, the publisher nor anyone known to them endorse the use of these patterns.

The Hospital Pattern

This is a fear inducing pattern that produces a fear of loss. It begins by describing a loss of something of great emotional value.

a) Did you ever know someone that went into a hospital and never came back?

b) it is amazing how often people just go, and never come back.

c) If you like what we have, remember that I could leave you, and never come back.

The operator would then capture the pieces into a nice little story and likely multiply the effect, using anchors.

Example said to lover:

a) "Did you hear about (insert famous person or acquaintance) *who went to the hospital for something* (anchor here) *and never came out?"*

b) "By the way, I had a doggie that I loved, and one day it just disappeared (use same anchor here with more intensity), (keep building value of doggie) *She was so good to me, she would wait for me after school, and she would just kiss me and knock me down, ever so gently. We would roll on the floor and play all kinds of games."*

Mind Control Language Patterns

c) "We would chase each other, she would fetch for me, she even slept in my room (what could you do with this?) *but then one day, I came looking for her, and she wasn't there. You have no idea what it feels like to lose someone like that* (anchor). *For days you look for her, you post posters, you post rewards. No matter what you do, it is over, gone out of your life* (anchor)."

The Depression Pattern

This pattern is very advanced, because it employs Values Elicitation and Anchoring.

The start of the pattern is to elicit the life values of the subject. In other words, the process begins with rapport and the operator asking, *"What's important to you in life?"* This will lead the subject finally to reveal whatever those values are and, for this example, let's say the subject answers "Family, religion and work," in that order of priority.

The operator will then ask the question, *"What are you not thinking about?"* This question will bring about a profound state of confusion in the subject, at which time the operator would covertly anchor the confusion with a touch or gesture.

The operator would then begin to talk about the subject's values of "Family, religion and work," and fire off the confusion anchor, linking confusion to these values, effectively nullifying them

The most malicious use of this or any "dark" pattern would be to have the subject to practice this response and have it effectively predetermined as an outcome. This might sound something like this:

"I'm not sure how well you can imagine thinking about *family, religion* and *work* and still having this feeling (firing anchor) in the future...from now on... but that's not something you have to think about consciously, as it takes place."

Consider now why this type of pattern is so malicious. When done effectively, anytime the subject thinks about what they used to have value in - family, religion and work - they now feel confused.

Elements of Dark NLP Patterns

There is an element of some Dark NLP patterns that, in itself, is not bad and is often used to help in an NLP therapeutic setting.

It is creating an anchor for "things that used to be true".

The hypnotic version of this would be to have the subject create a place or even a box in their mind that they put things that are no longer true for them. Then they can put habits, compulsions and cravings in the box, so that they no longer are true. The result is very effective and positive for the subject.

But what if the operator has them put things there that they value?

The effect would be much like the previous pattern.

Mind Control Language Patterns

Story Telling as Language Pattern

When anyone tells a vivid and compelling story, they are using metaphor to covertly influence and hypnotize. This is true, because a story is not personally about the listeners' lives, and therefore, the audience can absorb the messages, without feeling preached to. Also, in order for them to truly understand the story, they have to, at some level, feel the emotions of the characters. Because of the emotions a good story creates, stories are a great tool for mind control.

There are several good examples of this that can help a beginner understand the process of Mind Control. The first example is fairly common and happens any time someone reads a story or watches a movie and becomes so involved in the story line that they forget the fact they are involving themselves in a fiction.

In spite of the fact that they are maybe sitting on their couch reading or watching a TV show, they react as if they are in the story. In other words, they are being affected by what they are reading/watching AS IF IT WERE REAL.

This has been used by Mind Controllers all throughout history, and many shamanic cultures place the story teller as central person in their rituals.

To learn this skill, it is best that the controller first go into their history, and remember times when they were reading or watching a show and got so intensely involved that they lost track of time and began to care about the characters in the story.

What was it that made it so interesting?

How was it you forgot that you were at and 'got into the story'?

What emotions did the story involve?

By answering these questions, the controller can begin to understand what kinds of stories move them, and begin to craft stories they can tell that are equally involving.

How does one craft a story that delivers a covert message?

There are a few factors that one needs to consider and try to incorporate.

Mind Control Language Patterns

1. Tell a story with a character that is similar to the listener. The main character needs to have something that the listener can relate to, regardless if the main character is a turtle or a human being.

2. If telling the story orally (aloud), become involved, yourself. The more passion, energy and enthusiasm you can put in the story, the more the audience will react to it.

3. Lead off the subject, at times. The more one convolutes a story, the more the listener must involve themselves to follow it. Often you will hear a story begin like this:

> *"When I was little boy, my mother would send me over to her mother's house, my grandmother. And she would tell me stories from the old country. I've never heard these stories, except from here, so I don't know if she made them up or if they're just part of the folklore. She told me that when she was a little girl her cousin would tease her to go to the "The Witch's House" and talk to the lady they called "The Witch." The thing was that the witch didn't mind being called that, and my grandmother always approached the house scared, and every time The Witch would befriend her, take her in, tell her a story and she'd leave, always feeling better. Her friends told her that The Witch put a spell on her, which scared her every time, yet she would still go back for more.*
>
> *Well, one day The Witch told her a story about when she was a little girl and how she was always concerned about getting too close to the Black Lake. The Black Lake, they told her, was haunted and would pull young girls in from the shore and drown them, if they didn't take a certain path to the shore...."*

Just from this introduction, it is hard to tell who the story is really about - the person telling the story, the grandmother or the witch?

In order to understand it, the listener must forget who the story is about, and follow deeper and deeper into the story, eventually, losing themselves in it.

4) Design a message in the story. The message in the story can be like a moral of the story, like Aesop's Fables. The message can also be much

Mind Control Language Patterns

more covert. The covert message is one of emotion, meaning there is an emotion that the main character feels that motivates them. This emotion must be justified in the story. In doing this, the subject that hears the story can relate to the emotion. Remember a simple story, like Snow White...

Make up and tell a story that is convoluted, like the one above. Write it down, if you have to. Tell it to someone, and make impressionable young girls dream of a Prince Charming.

Exercise:

Observe how they respond. If you get a glassy-eyed stare in the midst of telling it, that is a sign of a hypnotic state induced by the story.

Other Variations of Story Telling

A testimonial is another example of story telling, because it is one person saying what happened to them with a certain product or service. It is used everywhere, from the religious practice of "witnessing" to TV commercials featuring both stars and ordinary people telling their story.

Exercise:

Make a list of all the times a testimonial has been used to sell a product or promote a service. Consider how you can do that with your outcome in mind. *Who can tell the story? What will they say?*

Mind Control Language Patterns

Magic Questions: The Cube

These were somewhat popular back in the good ol' days of the alt.seduction.fast newsgroup but have fallen out of favor in recent years, mostly due to the popularity of "The Cube."

Well, I got a fever, and the only prescription is Magic Questions. These are much easier to remember than The Cube, and can be done quickly. Best of all, it gives you insight into the person you're talking to. One time I had a girl answer the "beach" question by saying "I would run and hide!" I didn't spend more time on her.

The lead-in is simple. Just say your friend showed you an interesting personality test, or that you always ask people these questions, instead of exchanging resumes first. The questions are asked in order:

1. Visualize yourself in a white room. You're in a bed, and everything is white. How do you feel?

2. What is your favorite animal? What qualities do you see it as having?

3. What is your favorite color? How does it make you feel when you think about it?

4. Imagine yourself on a beach. Nobody is around, and the ocean is right in front of you. What do you do?

Now the answers:

1. This is how they view death and dying.

2. This is how their friends view them.

3. This is how they view themselves.

4. This is how they view sex.

I've turned around some of the coldest women I've ever encountered using this routine and conversation piece, so enjoy!

The pattern works, because the images they create are metaphors for aspects of the person's personality. The interesting thing about this patterns is that, much of the time, you can make anything they say mean anything you want it to mean, and it will generally be accepted, without question.

If you want a detailed description of "The Cube" process you can get the book "The Cube by by Annie Gottlieb and Slobodan D. Pesic.

Mind Control Language Patterns

Guerrilla War Linguistics

Dirty Tricks, Tactics and Put downs that Evade, Belittle and Disrupt any Argument.

It should be noted that these tactics are "dirty" in that they have nothing to do with reason or logic to win an argument. They are designed help person win an argument by putting the other person down or evading the subject.

You Wouldn't Understand

"That demands a response, but taking into account your background, education, and intelligence, I am not sure you would grasp it."

Basic Condescension

"This is key to the subject and I think even you can understand it."

"Even you should be able to get a handle on this next issue."

You're Young And Naive :

"That is what I used to think when I began learning."

"When you grow to an age of mental (emotional, spiritual) maturity you'll see how your way of thinking has really weighed you down."

"You're new here, aren't you?"

"Whoa! Did you just fall off the boat?"

Yeah, You Wish:

This s not to prove a point true or false, instead tries to imply that the individuals deepest wants have led them astray and sidesteps the issue itself. A strong desire can be used to show to have tainted an outcome of conclusion or and destroyed any objectivity. Thus it casts doubt on the legitimacy of a point. This is very close to the classic ad hominem fallacy: "you say that because you are a man."

"You support abortion because your hatred for like that is a result of emotional traumas during childhood."

Mind Control Language Patterns

"You were bullied as a child, were you?"

Disappearing Arguments

These are ways to make sure the unwanted subject disappears.

The Evasive Agreement

This is done by simply agreeing to one part of a persons objection.

Objection: *"As a gun lobbyist you represent the destroying of peoples lives."*

Answer: *"I must agree that lives destroyed by the progressive elimination of our civil rights is a horrible thing and there is no way I would stand for that."*

ATTENTION TO DETAIL

Instead of dealing with a comment or question directly, the idea here is to focus on some insignificant detail to evade the issue or buy time to think.

"Let's define just exactly what you mean by _____."

"Let's break it down word for word.."

"You used the pronoun 'the' but you really mean say "}'a'."

Twisted Context:

This one is very sneaky. The technique here is to intentionally misunderstand some part of what is stated and shift the focus to it instead of the subject. This forces other person into defending one insignificant part of the argument that was said out of hand.

"You're mixing up felling and thinking.. If you are feeling instead of thinking then you're stuck and can't learn."

"You said this happened in the era of Mo Tse Tung. Why are you so fascinated by chairman Mo? Are you supporting a cultural revolution."

I won't mention that ....

This is a strange way to come off as nice while saying things that would otherwise be considered rude.

Mind Control Language Patterns

"Have I ever brought up the I loaned you? Never! Have I ever embarrassed you or made you feel bad over it? Have I ever told you how much I need that money? No, I never have and I won't do it now."

"I'm not saying that all masons are evil..."
"I don't care if other people say you're boring..."
"I don't want to spend a lot of time on this, but (blah, blah, blah...)."

Trouble Making Questions:

The purpose of this argument is to throw the other person's competence in suspicion and change the subject at the same time. The person is asked a question to which they don't know the answer destroying their credibility and confidence. To be cruel the questioner and task the person by forcing them to answer a loaded question.

"You mentioned the constitution. Can you quote the preamble for us?"
"Do you realize the various rules of social etiquette you've just broken?" ["No."] "I'd be glad to explain them to you, but ...."

Any Intelligent Person Would...:

"Any intelligent person would agree with me that ...."
"Most people who disagree with this point haven't the experience to understand this point..."
"Of course there is a lot of debate on this subject, but all the authorities agree that ....

Low Blow:

"What was it your gay lover would say?"
"Weren't you saying the same thing just before you were indicted and went to rehab?"

Mind Control Language Patterns

Leading Questions:

This technique asks a leading question that plays on guilt or that drives the person to a common sense yes/no answer that supports the questioner's point of view. This is

Joining our church:
"Do you care about your families well being?" *["Well, yes!"]*
"Then I will see you at 10 am."

Support a political movement:
"Do you want a complete downfall of the America institution of democracy? Is that what you want?"

Join a Gym:
"Don't you care about your own body?"

The Flamboyant Challenge:

A tactic gives more emotional plea to a point or objection than is appropriate. Be ready for some overstated showmanship if you want to try this one. Melodrama and exaggeration becomes a central part of this tactic.

"Do you DARE question such an obvious point?"
"Get out of town! You can't REALLY expect me to support that fantasy?"

More Thinking, Less Feeling:

In this case you use the dichotomy between emotions and rationality. If they are emotional you attack their lack of rationality. If they are rational you attack their cold uncaring responses.

"You may be able to say it's reasonable but it's not rational. Your emotion is your only reason and it's completely irrational."

"You may be able to rationalize this and it completely evades the insensitivity to the emotional effect the issue has on people."

Mind Control Language Patterns

Creating a Conspiracy:

If the argument contains a novel or imaginative point, the questioner pushes the idea to a radical and unreasonable extreme. Whether it's realistic doesn't matter. The idea is to make it so extreme the other person will retreat and become defensive stopping the argument.

> *"So you think every masonic lodge is part of a conspiracy? What do you suggest?"*
> *"How is what you're saying different from paranoia?"*
> *"So everyone but you and your fellow believers are hiding behind a government conspiracy?"*

Create a Dead End

This is a way to preempt the continuation of an argument.

> *"I don't think we can go on until we test every possible consequence of your proposal."*
> *"Why are we arguing over what could be when we don't know all the facts. This is ridiculous."*

The Hammering Agreement

This tactic is simple and formulaic. It is a robot like response that is said so kindly and persistently the only option is to drop the subject . The key is to do it with completely supportive tone so as not to quickly agitate your opponant.

> *"I agree (nodding affirmatively) AND that is not what I was saying. (repeat your statement)..."*

Unacceptable Conclusion

This simply halts the conclusion and calling it unacceptable.

> *"In no way does your logic make sense."*
> *"Okay, you stated a series of facts. Yes, I can agree with them. But then you add them up to an irrational conclusion. The facts are there. The conclusion is way off."*

Mind Control Language Patterns

Delay Tactics

If, when put on the spot to answer a question or point, you come up blank, then delay tactics can buy time to dream up a response. These tactics are risky, because if you are not able to think of anything clever during the time you buy, you will be pinned even further.

Focus On The Answer

You must be able to think quickly on you feet to use these tactics and be able to endless "BS" your way around most any topic.

> *"Think about what you just said. Your answer can create some clarity on the topic. (Long pause) May I explain?"*

> *"Good question, hold on to your seat because there is some depth that only a few smart people like you can grasp.." (Pause, look thoughtfully as you think of what to say.)*

> *"I'm glad you asked. I can give you the short answer or the REAL one. Which do you want?"*

Focus on The Question

Same as above, only here the diversionary shift of focus is on the question.

> *"If you are asking that question and you are sincere about the answer you're going to get then please consider the nature of the question."*

> *"Consider that you are posing questions to the problem. It might be more productive to focus on the solution."*

> *"Give me a moment with what you said." (Long pause nodding affirmatively.) As I heard what you were saying the main points were..." (Restate the questions in various ways, delaying for time)*

Asking If They Truly Want An Answer

This one is designed to make them shut up and feel on the defensive.

Mind Control Language Patterns

"Most people ask a question because they want to know the answer. It seems as though you are just asking to prove your point and that you don't want to hear ... or aren't truly willing to hear... what the answer could be."

Throw Doubt on The Question or Comment
This is a variation of the Sleight of Mouth patterns.

"Who told you that would be the best question to ask?"
"Have you thought how asking that presupposes what you're not thinking about?'
"Have you considered how the opposite might benefit you?"

Confusion Comment
A complex statement that paralyzes the brain.

"Consider what you are not thinking about right now."
"I really don't doubt that you can't not completely change your thoughts that way."
"Your problem is that you are thinking in a linear versus configurational framework."
"I'm not sure if I fail to disagree with that or not."

Baffle Them With BS
A bureaucrat will to this to no end. It is basically BS with big words that seem so sophisticated as to be unintelligible. Include a few words that appear to pertain to the subject. Without saying truly anything it can sound very impressive. It's important that it be sprinkled with simple commands for attention like "Stay with me on this." and "Keep your focus this is important." Done well it can actually seem as if you made a point.

"In view of the configurations of financial institutions and and current tax laws, and noting the need to mitigate the desertions of world leaders toward their own localized financial considerations, there are important steps that each of us can do to in order to put things right."

Mind Control Language Patterns

Boomerang Question
Here you don't answer the question, instead you ask the questioner to answer it.

"I think you have your own answer to that question. So what answer would you pose?"

The Old Geezer Delay Tactic
This is similar to the "Baffle Them With BS" tactic except that it involves story telling. Imagine an Old Geezer hearing your question and having it trigger a flood of mostly irrelevant stories with no foreseeable end in sight.

"That reminds me when we were hunkered down avoiding an ambush in the middle east. You could smell death on the other side of the door. My buddy, Lex, was trained as a sniper but the problem was we could hardly find enough room to aim, point and shoot. He once demonstrated his marksmanship by shooting the flagpole cable off an enemy encampment...."

Being Over Literal
Here you take their words and remove all figurative references in your reply.

Example: {How do you sleep at night?}
I lie prone with my eyes closed.

{What is the difference between these two people doing the same job for different pay?}
"I would guess the difference has to do with what they are paid."

Any Answer Will Do
This tactic is to use the question, whatever it was, to be a sounding board for the answer or statement you want to give. They question and answer may seem completely unrelated to each other.

Mind Control Language Patterns

Classic Redefine
This is a Sleight of Mouth tactic where the entire issue is redefined to suit your answer

"It is not a question of (this) or (that), but rather it is an issue of (insert your issue here.)"

"By focusing on [X] you're avoiding the bigger/real/important issue of..."

["Are you for or for or against (name issue) ?"] "I don't think the issue is being for or against (issue). The real issue is (insert your issue here). I propose that we...."

Two Separate Issues
This tactic allows you to divide the other persons facts and conclusions into two separate issues and refocus where you want to go.

"My personal life is one issue, getting the results you need is another. Let's focus on accomplishing something positive. Agreed"
"We could discuss that topic or we could focus on (name topic)."

Hypothetical Insult:
This tactic is mean and devious because it allows you to insult and then say "I'm not saying you're a ____."

"Hypothetically, if I knew for a fact that you have no idea about that which you speak, what would my best answer be?"

Hidden Insult

"I have to compliment you on answering that far beyond your education level."
"You look good. Your dress didn't offend anyone today."
"Congratulations on not saying anything stupid at the meeting."

Mind Control Language Patterns

Inactive Listening

Active listening is a constructive communication method where you acknowledge what the other person has said by restating it back to them. Inactive listening allows you to restate what was said but pervert it to you own ends.

"So you're saying that institutionalized torture is appropriate for national security."

"So what you're saying is ... (give a perverted interpretation of their statement)."

Label and Oversimplify

As a general rule when you label something you make it real. With this tactic you take whatever the other person has said and put it in a figurative box to throw away.

"Your reasoning falls into an area of non-Euclidean thought."

Look Into Their Hearts

This tactic is a polite way to tell the other person that you know more, and therefore better, about what that person believes, thinks and feels.

"That hurt me deeply. I know you're not the type of person to say that."

"I don't doubt you mean well. Your heart is in the right place. I even believe you've given this some deep thought and deep inside I know you're better than to hold on to that belief."

Confabulation

This is, in short, a lie about a previous event. It's only use is to put the other person on the defensive or confuse them. A good way to start is to bring up an insignificant event and misrepresent it.

"You've never lied to me? You once told me you hated chocolate."

Mind Control Language Patterns

"You are always changing your mind. You did it last month when you said you wanted to eat out. How can I believe anything you are telling me?"

Quote an Authoritative Study

This can be a last resort. One simply refers to a bogus study and makes up statistics and authorities to add credibility to what they say. There is a risk that someone will call you on your bluff. If this happens the response is to add more BS to the study and add fake credibility.

"The Meninger institute did a comprehensive study that proves..."

"Psychological studies at Yale University and shown a different conclusion."

Truisms, Slogans and Exaggerations

This is a very annoying tactic that relies on wild gestures, crazy behavior in response to a comment or question.

"Buy low. Sell high. It's all about the bottom line." Do this while looking like a mad man.

Upset The Cart

This cruel tactic is designed to upset the questioner and then redirect their response to justify your outcome.

"I'll tell you my answer but you're so emotionally unstable you wouldn't grasp my intent and it would be a waste of time." {The other person gets upset} "Now, you are proving my point. Going wild. Answering your question was a bad idea."

Referring To Their Response

This can be truly annoying. What you do is take any physical reaction or response and use it as proof that they are wrong and you are right.

Mind Control Language Patterns

"You can sit there biting your lip in that chair slouched over that way and it only proves that you know how weak your argument is."

"Keep trying to look at me with that blank gaze and you and I both know how hard it is to admit you're wrong."

Use a Useful Quotation

This is a stall tactic in which you use a quote, real or imagined to take up some time.

"The bible says that if you have the faith of a mustard seed you can move mountains. Let me ask you is your faith enough to put aside your judgment and consider my position?"

"My grandfather was a judge and he always said..."

Fast Thinking

This is about giving your response a sense of authority. This done by answer fast and with as much detail as possible.
{How can you feel that others will support your idea?}

"A comprehensive study surveying 82 random respondents showed that 77% would support it. Seventy Seven percent!"

Throwing a Fit

Imagine asking a question or posing an argument and know you right. Using this tactic the response would be an emotional tirade that is complete with sobbing, long pauses, and a cold and hateful gaze. In general making it as uncomfortable as possible. This response puts anyone on edge and warns them to step lightly the next time they consider the topic.

Rapid Fire

The purpose here is to provide more attacks to the other persons argument then they can defend and to do it in rapid fire, nit picking the smallest detail.

Mind Control Language Patterns

"What do mean by 'THE answer'... Define what you mean by time. Where did you get your fact? Who told you that detail?"

Attacking Their Identity

Here you question whether the questioner is the type of person to believe that.

"Is that the type of person you see yourself as?"

Listen to me!

This gives you two reactions. The first is if they comment on anything you said with *"You don't listen to anything I say."* The second response is if they do sit and listen and comment *"You didn't hear a word I said."*

Mind Control Language Patterns

Meta Programs As Language Patterns

Meta Programs are ways that we sort information. Everyone has their own method of organizing their thoughts. When you know how someone sorts information, and you present your ideas using their sorting process, then they respond very favorably to it. Understanding Meta Programs adds a depth to language patterns, because now you are able to tailor your language patterns to more perfectly fit the person you are working with.

What follows is a list of eighteen of the most useful meta programs borrowed from the book "Perfected Mind Control," with added information to help you apply them as language patterns.

1) Criteria Which Lead to Values

Criteria is a list of what is important within a certain context. In order to find one's criteria, the question is asked, *"What do you want in an X?"* You should get a list of three to six criteria.

To turn this into a language pattern, you must focus in on their criteria and what their criteria gives them. Fulfilling a criteria will NOT consistently convince someone to buy your idea, product or service. Criteria are simply their first surface level response to any context.

Values are an extension of criteria and have strong emotions attached. When you fulfill a value, you trigger these strong emotions. To get to someone's values, you start with their criteria and ask, *"What's important about criteria?"* With that, you'll get a response, but this is usually not the true value, but you'll be getting close.

With that information, which we'll call "criteria2," you'll ask further, *"What's important about criteria2?"* With their next answer, criteria3, it may still not be reach their value, so you can ask again, *"What's important about criteria3?"*

As an alternative to asking, *"What's important about X,"* you may also ask, *"When you have X fully and completely, what does that give you that's important?"*

Mind Control Language Patterns

Often, it is then that they will tell you their value. You will know it by a subtle, or not so subtle, expression of emotion, when they answer that third question. When you hit a real emotion, then you've hit pay dirt, and you'll know simply by paying attention. This is where you must be acutely sensitive to the other person's response, in order to notice this emotional response. When you hear their value, remember the exact words they use.

It is very simple to use this answer as a language pattern. All you need to do is work in the exact words they use when sharing your idea, product or service. By doing this, you link your idea, product or service with their value. This process is much more powerful than you might first imagine.

2) Direction

When asking about criteria and values, you will discover that people choose them, either because they bring them good things they want, or spare them from bad things they don't want. To determine which motivates them more ask, *"What will having* (their criteria) *do for you?"*

The response will either be a TOWARDS response, with words like *attain, achieve, goals, include, accomplish, solutions* or an AWAY FROM response, with words like *avoid, get away from, evade,* and *exclude.*

The importance of this as a language pattern is to make sure that you fulfill their Direction meta program. In other words, if they answer your question of *"What will having* (their criteria) *do for you?"* with, *"It gets me away from the noise at work,"* then it would be an error to emphasize "silence" instead of "freedom from noise." The person's statement describes moving away from noise - not going towards silence. There is a difference.

3) Source

This will help you to provide them with the type of evidence they best respond to.

"How do you know that you have done a good job in _____? Do you know it inside, or does someone have to tell you?"

Mind Control Language Patterns

Their response will be one of the following:

( ) INTERNAL - Knows inside self – here you would describe how they can just "know" that your idea/product is good.

( ) MOSTLY INTERNAL, SOME EXTERNAL - This will mean that, while you intend to affirm their inner state of certainty, you should also provide some external evidence.

( ) EXTERNAL – Told by Others – Give them lots of testimonial evidence.

( ) MOSTLY EXTERNAL, SOME INTERNAL - Give them lots of testimonial evidence, and elicit their own inner state of certainty.

4) Reason

With this meta program, your subject will tell you, not merely the reason, but the process of their decision making.

"Why did you choose your current/most-recent _____?"

( ) OPTIONS – Criteria, Look for other ways, possibilities

( ) MOSTLY OPTIONS, SOME PROCEDURE

( ) PROCEEDURE – Necessities, Facts, The Way

( ) MOSTLY PROCEDURES, SOME OPTIONS

Depending on their answer, you will have to tailor your presentation to this meta program. Someone who uses a procedures method will not be convinced if you make an options presentation. Likewise, a person using the options meta program will get very bored of hearing a procedures meta program.

Procedures will sound like a long story about how they came to their decision. Options will describe the choices they made and why they chose what they did.

5) Relationship

Mind Control Language Patterns

To determine a how a person sorts information using this meta program, they are often shown three coins of the same denomination - two as heads and one as tails - and asked the following question, *"What is the relationship between these three coins?"* Note that they are NOT asked, *"How are they the same?"* nor *"How are they different?"* - but the **relationship**.

Other questions you can ask are:

"What it the relationship between what you're doing this year and what you were doing last year?"

"On average, how long have you stayed on a job/in a relation-ship?"

( ) SAMENESS – Same thing, No Change, Similar

( ) SAMENESS /w EXCEPTION

( ) DIFFERENCE - Different, change, New, Unique

( ) DIFFERENCE /w EXCEPTION

As they describe the relationship, this will tell you how to present things that are comparisons. So if they respond with sameness, you would describe all the things that are the same; if differences, then you describe all the things that are different.

6) Convincer and Convincer Demonstration

These two meta programs put together create an unstoppable way to convince someone of ANYTHING.

Quite simply, all you need to know is how they know something is good and over what time do they have to experience it.

"How do you know that a _____ is a good?"

( ) SEE

( ) HEAR

Mind Control Language Patterns

( ) DO

( ) READ

Thus if they have to see something, in order to be convinced, you show them. If they need to hear about something, you have people tell them, and so on.

This is followed by the next meta program.

7) Convincer Demonstration

How often do they have to demonstrate being good to you, before you are convinced?

( ) _____ TIMES

( ) _____ LENGTH OF TIME

( ) AUTOMATIC

( ) CONSISTENT

8) Primary Sort

People make decisions to do things, based on what attracts them to it. There are five possible things that people are attracted to when making a decision - **people, places, things, activities** and *information*.

Tell me about a vacation that you really enjoyed or what you think would be your ideal vacation. What did/would you like about it?

( ) PEOPLE

( ) PLACE

( ) THINGS

( ) ACTIVITY

( ) INFORMATION

Mind Control Language Patterns

When you have the answer to this question, you can then make your presentation based on the people, places, things, activities or information that most appeals to them.

9) Style

This meta program indicates how someone relates to others, given certain situations. This one is useful with the context of coordinating actions and activities.

Tell me about a _____ in which you were happiest (a one time event).

( ) INDEPENDENT – I, Sole responsibility, Myself, Alone

( ) PROXIMITY – With Others, But In Control

( ) COOPERATIVE – All of Us, With Others, We, Share Responsibility

10) Chunk Size

Some people want and need the details of a subject to understand it. Others consider themselves to be "big picture" types, who need to look at things from a distance. You can notice the first group of people, those who need specifics, at the front of a lecture, feverishly taking notes, trying to get all the information. Those people who want the general information will be sitting or standing at the back of the room, trying to soak it all in, and get a feel for the information.

One way to determine this meta program is to ask, *"To really learn something in a lecture - is the best seat for you up front* (SPECIFIC) *or in the back of the room?"* (GENERAL).

This meta program is also revealed by how they speak:

Mind Control Language Patterns

SPECIFIC: will talk with and about sequences. Extra modifiers used. They use proper nouns.

GENERAL: Simple sentences, few modifiers. No sequence, Steps left out. No proper nouns.

11) Modal Operators

What did you say to yourself this morning, when you decided to get up?

(Circle one: Can, Have To, Must, Want, Gotta, etc.)

Modal operators are the words that people use to motivate themselves into action. If you use the words that they use on themselves to put them into action, they are more likely to comply.

12) Stress Response

Tell me about a _____ situation that gave you trouble.

( ) THINKING

( ) FEELING

( ) CHOICE

This will be of use, only if you are to describe the negatives that they want to avoid.

13)Attention Direction

Do they react to others' changes in moods, or do they ignore others' changes around them?

( ) SELF

( ) OTHERS

14) Values

In the context of life - what's important to you?

List 9 or 10 things.

Rank them in order of importance.

Mind Control Language Patterns

15)

If you could fantasize aloud for a moment about the ideal _____ for you, what would it be?

16)

What do you look forward to in a _____?

These last two questions will help you formulate the positive aspects of what you want to persuade the other person to do or buy.

Mind Control Language Patterns

Using Emotions to Persuade

Warning:

In order to make the point of how emotions are used to persuade, I have two outcomes in mind. The first is to demonstrate subtle emotional elicitation. The second is to encourage you to invest in learning more about persuasion. As a result, you might think I am being overtly manipulative. I AM! Because, in order for persuasion to occur, it must happen within a context. The context is: Learning and sharpening your persuasion skills.

Emotions

When first learning persuasion skills, it's often the goal of the initiate to make people do certain things that are in the initiate's interests. They may consider simply putting the subject in a trance and telling them to do things for them. That reality is rare and the learner of persuasion will quickly find out that people are not motivated by thoughts, but by emotions. Through the elicitation of emotions in the subject, the persuader will get their outcome.

In persuasion literature, they are referred to as "discrete emotions," because they are elicited and felt subjectively, without an outward expression. Most persuasive writing and speeches appeal to several emotions, both positive and negative. When you read a persuasive sales letter, you can begin to list the emotional states they are trying to elicit.

Likewise, when you are persuading someone, be mindful of their emotional states and the emotions you are trying to elicit.

With that in mind, I'd like to demonstrate, in writing, the persuasive use of both positive and negative emotions.

The Need to Learn Persuasion

Mind Control Language Patterns

Pride - Let me first begin by saying "Thank you." Of all the people in the world, you've taken the steps that have brought you here to learn more about persuasion. That translates as you being a single fraction of a percent of all the people in the world who value themselves enough to know that learning persuasion skills is absolutely vital to your success and well being. Before you read any further, take a second to acknowledge your efforts in getting this far, because there are too many moments that pass us by when we don't take pride in what we've done.

Fear - I've been studying persuasion for almost a decade. The sad fact is that there are some people who know these skills and would use them on anyone, regardless of the possible negative effect it might cause. Some people have referred to these as "Dark Side" NLP skills, and I can tell you from personal experience that they do exist! I also know that the only way to protect yourself from any of these malicious processes and language patterns is to know about them. Yes, knowledge is your only defense against the most wicked people who would even think to use them.

Anger -I've seen the results of these destructive language patterns. They are devious, because most people don't even know they've happened. They live life half-heartedly, with no purpose, because someone meant to hurt them! If you know of anyone using these language patterns and NLP skills to injure, you have every right to act and stop them!

Hope -But there is a bright side to all of this. Persuasion skills, like the ones I teach, are there to benefit you and everyone who knows them. Using these skills, I've seen people overcome life-long phobias and land million dollar contracts. You can use these skills just as easily to land the perfect job, meet your ideal romantic partner and end what may, at times, seem like an endless cycle of just trying to pay the bills. Knowing these persuasion skills and how to apply them, you can benefit your life and the lives of others.

Envy - Okay, it's true we want all of that. What sane person doesn't? I have a friend who easily uses the persuasion skills I teach to get everything he wanted. He's happy, he's loved, he's proud of what he's accomplished, and every time we meet, he's eager to tell me, or anyone, about the richness that life has to offer. He also wants everyone to know that they can have what they want, too.

Some people will tell you that he's a freak, an abnormally happy person, but his message is that he got it largely due to his hard work and knowledge of how the mind works. For him, persuasion has become easy.

Guilt - He has a less positive side, too. There are some times when he's taken people aside and reminded them how much they haven't really lived up to what they could do. He makes a good point. We each may have started with an idea or ideal, but we stopped and never finished it. There is something to be said about squarely facing your shortcomings. You may have shown an interest in persuasion - but how much have you really dedicated yourself to learning and using it?

For most people, the answer is, "Not much."

When you're faced with that reality, it can really eat away at how you think of yourself. That's a burden I don't want you to ever face again.

Sadness - It can be like we've really lost something. Lost a hope for our lives. By realizing that we haven't lived up to what we could be, most people are compelled to act. Compelled to do something... anything, rather than feel the real burden and misery of losing control of life.

Happiness/Joy - The one great comfort of all of this is that there is a solution that comes by just taking a few simple steps. One of them is making a decision to learn persuasion skills, by investing in your first persuasion product. When you do that, you know you're doing something right.

Improving yourself is the one act no one can take away, and it will be with you for the rest of your life.

Relief - When you do take those steps, a burden will be lifted. If you could imagine the freedom of having the time to enjoy the things that you want, take vacations and participate in the social activities you've always loved, that's what you'll have for yourself, by becoming a life-long student of persuasion skills.

Anticipation -You've read this far, so I know you're showing some interest, and there is a lot to look forward to.

Think about it. Instead of looking back on what you could have done but didn't, you can start to look forward to making life changing decisions. Let me paint a picture for you of what you can look forward to when you become a real master of this type of influence and mind control.

Every day you learn and apply new skills. You learn how to get more of what you want from others and have them like you for it. You feel unstoppable.

As you learn these skills, your life will change, as well. You'll find that you're more confident, relaxed and able to talk to anyone anytime.

Regret - My friend, Tony Robbins, points out that, near the end of life, most people find it way TOO   easy to look back and see the opportunities we could have chosen, but didn't. It's the things we didn't do that we regret more than what we chose to do. There is an opportunity right now that could change everything for you... and you could pass it up, and regret it forever.

Let me just stop right here and point out that no one really knows how much time we have on this earth. Because we don't know, we think it's limitless, but it's not. You have no idea how many full moons you'll see in your life - maybe 20, maybe only five. How many times will you see a butterfly spread its wings and fly? Maybe 10 times? Maybe less. Maybe more.

Opportunities are like that, too.

When you commit yourself to learning persuasion skills, you've made the decision that will positively affect you and everyone around you. Don't walk away, and make a choice to live only half a life.

Mind Control Language Patterns

Every moment is an opportunity, and using your knowledge of persuasion, you'll be able to take advantage of opportunities you never knew how to before.

Conclusion

The list of emotions used is by no means exhaustive, and I encourage you to explore how to use discrete emotional appeals to persuade, influence and negotiate.

Let me first recognize that a few readers may have read this far and felt unnerved, irritated or coerced and even compelled to invest in persuasion products. That is not the point. Emotions play a powerful part in any persuasion context, no matter how subtle. It will benefit any would-be persuasion expert to pay attention to the emotions they see and the emotions they attempt to elicit.

Mind Control Language Patterns

Using Mind Control to Create an Addiction (dark)

With all the paranoia of mind control and how NLP can be (and is) used to "mess with peoples' heads," it's time to pull the cat out of the bag and let people know exactly what is possible. For example, can you create an addiction in someone using NLP?

Yes, you can.

Before you learn the steps to do it and how to protect yourself, let me give you two warnings. First, don't do this to people, unless you are giving them a compulsion for something they want that will be good for them - like exercise and healthy foods. Anything else, and it may seem fun to think about, but leave it at that. Only think about it, don't do it. It's just not a nice thing to do to people. Second, to do this you have to be very good at NLP.

Start by eliciting what is called the NLP submodalities of a compulsion a person has. You can do this by asking what are some things they have compulsions for, like chocolate, and then asking, *"As you feel that compulsion, what sort of images is your mind making? Where do you see those pictures? How big are the images? Color or black and white? "* and so on.

Then begin to describe what you want them to have a compulsion /addiction for, in exactly the same way. Describe the new compulsion as being seen in the same place, etc. One doesn't need any more detail than that. It's more than enough to experiment with. Using this pattern, a person can create a compulsion for drugs, sex, money, perfection, driving fast - you name it; however, one can also create compulsions for exercise, punctuality, orderliness and many so-called "good" things.

Powerful compulsions have a strong pleasure/pain dynamic. As an example, a sexual compulsion may have a pleasure/guilt or pleasure/fear dynamic. Food compulsions may have a depression/relief dynamic.

Without going into details, this is enough information to engineer a very powerful compulsion.

Using this methodology, it is possible create a compulsion in someone, so that they compulsively want to make you happy. While some might not consider this a completely "dark" application, it is not focused on the other person's happiness and well-being, so it cannot be considered "light," either.

To make this "compulsion to want to make me happy" complete, you should also consider including in "happy" other emotions such as "satisfied," "at peace," "loved" and others, because simply "happy" may not be the best emotion, given the situation.

There are ways to prevent someone from covertly creating a compulsion in *you*. First, be aware of the mental and emotional states that people are asking you to describe, and be on guard when they start to talk about compulsions. If you suspect someone has helped covertly create an unwanted compulsion in you (good luck), the compulsion can be undone with what is called the meta yes/meta no process.

In **Meta Yes/Meta No,** you'll start by thinking of something unrelated to the compulsion that you would say "no" to. Think of that item, and bring up the very strong feeling, and repeatedly say, "No" in a firm and congruent manner. Practice it until the "No!" and the feeling are deeply linked to one another. The next step is to begin saying, "No!" repeatedly to the compulsion, and do it with the same energy and conviction as when you started the process.

Mind Control Language Patterns

The Voice Roll

The voice roll is a way of speaking that is very common among public speakers, and especially common with preachers giving sermons.

The voice roll is a way of speaking that has specific rhythm. The rhythm creates a hypnotic effect with a majority of the audience. The reason why is that the rhythm, itself, becomes unconsciously anticipated and thus the listener follows the rhythm.

The specifics of the rhythm is about pausing briefly 45 to 60 times a minute, or about once a second.

Here is an example of the voice roll with (...) representing the brief pause:

"There is pattern... of unique thinking ... that allows us... to see how each of us... can create such power... create such influence... that people will follow... Now... think of it!... it is all in how you think... that propels others... to follow... it is as if you have behind you... a force of will... And that is what it is... A force of Will!! So think about what you want... Think about how... you want to affect people... Imagine that you CAN... and you are on your way..."

Another way of setting a rhythm is to pace it according to the breath; breathing normally and only speaking on the exhale. This creates a unique pattern that is unconscious. To understand it, consider what happens when we breathe with emotion. When we feel excitement, the emphasis is on the inhale. We sigh with relief. By pausing on the inhale, the speaker is stimulating the part of the unconscious mind that inhales with anticipation, and by speaking on the exhale, unconsciously providing relief.

When speaking to an individual, the speaker would pace the breathing of the listener. Speaking to a group is much easier, as the speaker does not have to pace anyone. The process, alone, will allow the audience to follow the inhale-exhale/anticipation-relief pattern.

Exercise:

Take a book, and before reading aloud, notice your breath. Breathe the same way as you read aloud, only speaking on the exhale.

Mind Control Language Patterns

October Man:
October Man Sequence

(What follows is my observations on the seduction course called, "The October Man Sequence" no attempt has been made to edit/correct or improve any part of this since it was first created.)

This was written in response to Swingcat's book, called, The October Man.

Ok here goes ... Are you familiar with Tension Loops? If you have Swinggcat's book it's about that story of the cat named girl-george ... Pain/Pleasure/Pain Push/Pull kinda thing.

...Thats the GP version, in the context of October Man, you have to amp up the pain and the pleasure ... Every time you talk about anything pleasurable, you anchor it to you physically or just by special gestures. I do it by a unique stare ... Every time you go to Pain, you anchor it away by gesturing, or just looking away ... Remember to really bring out her Pleasurable states by patterning or just Trance Hi-Jack or create that into filters - SRT style just as used in the new SS model ... You can do SRT on the environment or create those dark filters on the world or others etc... Really work on the positive states, stack them up, multi-modal anchoring etc... You can also use kinesthetic DHE panels/sliding anchors for pain (others) and pleasure (to you) on the arm or leg or objects even and stack it with other techniques. This is the crucial part, when she's in such a high bliss, you have to immediately contrast it with something really Painful/Disgusting/Traumatic and all the uppermost amped up negative states you can bring out. As I told you, this will give you headaches, as you must really explore those pain submodalities and make them real... If you tone it down, its just standard tension loops like, "Oh my god I love you" but pushing her away. That, in itself, is a roller coaster ride, and for daily Sarges, this will do... For industrial strength Mindfucking, Tension Loops from Hell is gonna do it... Imagine the most intense flaming ball of fire, then in a heartbeat freezing it, till it's a ball of DRY ICE, reigniting it back up to a fireball, and so forth ... the contrast has to be that intense and RAPID FIRE, minimize or no fluff talk, if possible ... Just practicing this alone is a big mindfuck and

Mind Control Language Patterns

does take a toll on you, after a few minutes ... Important thing is to learn to desensitize or disassociate in the PAIN stuff, while making them real! By now, you'd have already noticed the FRACTIONATION, you'd have already noticed that at each pass YOU ARE BUILDING RESPONSE POTENTIAL on both polarities ... Each pass, you fractionate the pain, so it's intensifying, while also intensifying the pleasure back to you ... I don't know if you can consider going to the Pain part, fractionation, but it does make them more scared to go to pain and more reactive, when you go to the pleasure part ... This kind of talking really sounds weird, so you can use the context of this being a survey from a psychology class or something ... If they don't want to open up their past, you do quotes ... You do routines, just to get in there.

Here's the part that you already know ... Are you familiar with Time-Lines, Change History Pattern or the "February Man" by Erickson? Same principle, you visit her in her timeline, in the future (future projections on the Mystery Method) or in the past, and evoke the things that were painful then ... Work it, then be like The Knight In Shining Armor (this part is Style's version), protector and how things could have been better, if you were there to shield her, bring her to safety, etc ... Those periods in her life when she needed someone, and nobody was there etc ... In the pleasurable moments, you can "steal" them and make them stronger, or many times better, had you been there ... Create artificial histories, which I know would already come easy for you, standard change history stuff ... Nothing special. When in10se emailed me (not about this specifically), he said something profound, which I may or may not get correctly ... Unconscious Incompetence I guess ... Anyway, he said that the people he personally saw do these dark type patterns correctly were Steve P/Mark Cunnignham/RJ/Swinggcat and himself... Something about shared explorations, or shared trance and putting in strong intent! I understand it, but I don't know if that's the understanding he wanted to convey ... If you're gonna use this, please avoid the Time-Line part ... The Tension Loop from hell is enough to get you fast connections ... It time distorts them automatically, and she feels safe with you ... Don't do this in situations with a lot of stimuli or distractions like clubs etc.

The hospital pattern below is an example of how Pain/Pleasure works ...

Try also the "Door Pattern."

Mind Control Language Patterns

The Hospital Pattern:

a) Did you ever know someone that went into a hospital and never came back?

b) It's amazing how often people just go and never come back.

c) If you like what we have, remember that I could leave you and never come back.

Now you just capture the pieces into a nice little story. If you can use touch or smell, the anchors are that much more powerful.

Example said to lover:

a) *"Did you hear about* (insert famous person or acquaintance) *who went to the hospital for something* (anchor here) *and never came out?"*

b) *"By the way, I had a doggie that I loved, and one day it just disappeared* (use same anchor here with more intensity), (keep building value of doggie) *She was so good to me, she would wait for me after school, and she would just kiss me and knock me down, ever so gently. We would roll on the floor, and play all kinds of games."*

c) *"We would chase each other, she would fetch for me, she even slept in my room* (what could you do with this?), *but then one day, I came looking for her, and she wasn't there. You have no idea what it feels like to loose someone like that* (anchor). *For days, you look for her, you post posters, you post rewards. No matter what you do, it's over, gone out of your life* (anchor)."

Clearly, **tonality, certainty** and **body language** will have much to do with your results.

"The last thing I remember was when I left, and she kissed me, (anchor) *and I never saw her again. I wouldn't wish that (anchor) on anyone."*

Mind Control Language Patterns

"I sure enjoy you (fire anchor), *and I am having a blast getting to know you. I know you'll miss me."* (fire anchor)

―――――――

The anchor will be set, and you can use it anytime. The power of the pattern is in creating a solid story - use voice, touch and any other compound anchors that you can.

By the same token, you can create:

The broken window pattern

The stolen art pattern

The solar eclipse pattern

The lost shoe pattern

The lost ring pattern

The final goodbye pattern

All of these are only limited by your imaginations.

As the "major" of hypnosis says, "Do the drill, get the skill".

=======Gemini Pattern=======

Ok guys, remember to do the necessary anchoring and self points and substitute hypnotic languaging, as you see fit. The more defined the modules are, the more real they become ...

The Gemini Pattern:

a) *"Most people don't realize there are actually two women inside the woman. There's the culturally/socially programmed woman* (build on this) *i.e. roles she has to play like Debbie the mother, Debbie the employee etc ..."*

b) *"But then there's the natural woman, who has passions, fantasies, sexual feelings, amazing possibilities, the most exciting memories, the*

Mind Control Language Patterns

kinds of things you wouldn't want your best friends to know about."
(build on this)

<Safety module>

"(Because of the roles she has to play according to society), a person has to lock that place away, to keep it safe, and yet it's (the natural woman) inside, just waiting to emerge ... Waiting to be released."

<Access module >

"What is it about the way certain people affect us that causes us to think of THIS SPECIAL PERSON in that special place, to hear this voice, to feel this presence, see this face from that spot."

<Dark Sun module>

"In such a way that no matter how we TRY to deny that desire to act, it takes on a life of its own, compelling, vivid, real."

<Internal Voice module>

"Where this voice inside says, 'YES! I want to step into that special place with this special person, and explore anything that we can both make real!'" (another definition - LOVE)

<Awakening Parts module>

"What would it be like for a person to just right now, feel all those hidden parts and desires, and wakeup hungry, ready and alive!"

<Act Now module>

"Realizing this is the moment, right here RIGHT NOW! A chance to move in to a nude erection (new direction). The thing about them (nude erections) is that it's not just enough to ponder them, instead you've got

Mind Control Language Patterns

to reach out, grab hold of them, take it all in as far as it will go - make it a part of who you are."

Freud said - "We are made so that we can only derive IN10SE pleasure from a contrast." Basically, this is "Parts" technique. There are several reasons why this is powerful ... Remember the "Sleight of Mouth" technique of reframing something from Generalized into Specifics?

Example:

Someone has the belief that they can't talk to a girl, because she is too beautiful.

Reframe: "Who, specifically, says you can't talk to her? What, specifically, makes you unable to talk to her? etc ..."

The key concept is that, when you break something into PARTS, you also break apart resistance.

So, for example, The Gemini Pattern is about a truism ... it's a theme. But it also breaks someone into PARTS, i.e. There is a PART of you that feels THIS way and wants to do THIS.

Good PARTS techniques also use PACING.

For example,

"Yes, there is a part of you that wants to hold back ... that wants to appear conservative and follow society's rules for the way that you SHOULD act ... but there is also a PART of you that wants to give in to what you really want ... what your body feels ... what you REALLY want to do ..."

I have a theme called "The Shadow and the Rising Sun" that uses PARTS as well.

Mind Control Language Patterns

The Shadow and the Rising Sun Pattern:

a) *"You know, I was thinking about something the other day ... about polarities ... about the whole concept of the Yin and Yang ... about hot and cold ... black and white ... light and darkness. And how opposites are really the same thing ... just varying degrees on the same spectrum ... of possibilities ... and how one is defined in relation to the other ... and how there are no absolutes."*

b) *"And then I remembered something that a psychologist friend of mine said once ... She said, "I have to go feed my shadow" ... and I wasn't quite sure what she meant at the time, until I read something by Jung."*

c) *"We are born completely whole, and it isn't until we learn what our current culture tells us what is good and what is bad that we start to both repress and express these parts of ourselves."*

d) *"He said that everyone has a Shadow ... a hidden side ... a place of forbidden desire. This is that part of you that you hide from the rest of the world ... maybe even from yourself ... where you can experience and imagine these thoughts ... these thoughts that you don't tell anyone about ... where you really want to experience all the excitement of this moment ... to let go of all the things that had been holding you back before ... to just let go ... experience all that life offers you now. The Shadow is a good thing, he believed, because it brings a sense of balance."*

e) *"Now, this sense of balance is very important because the concept that whatever you repress grows and begins to spill over into other parts of your life. If your shadow is repressed, it grows and grows ...until it just takes you over completely. Jung said it was like the Rising Sun ... because in the morning, as the Sun rises in the sky ... it gets higher and higher ... closer and closer, to the highest point in its path (midlife) ... until at mid-day it changes polarity completely... and everything that was once true has now changed... and now the opposite is true... and the sun goes down. This was the concept behind mid-life crisis."*

f) *"So balance, then, is a good thing, and Jung believed that the first part of our lives is about separation from the shadow, while the latter part of our lives is about integration with the shadow and about being whole."*

g) *"Now what if you were to see your shadow right in front of you, and talk to it - what would it say?"*

h) *"Now, what if you were to step into your shadow right now, and see the world through the eyes of your shadow ... What would that say about the person that you were before - and what does this say about who you are now?"*

Now, let me just tell you - **Symbolic Morphology** is the foundation and STARTING point for the October Man.

Symbolic Morphology evolved out of Symbol Fractionation, which was the version that RJ used.

So in symbolic morphology, you basically elicit a body sensation ... almost like eliciting a state or a value ... except that it's a BODY sensation ... a feeling. Remember that what you NAME, you bring to life ... what you DESCRIBE becomes real.

You have the person describe where this feeling is, what it feels like, what they do to make it happen ... etc.

And then you give it a COLOR. You turn it into a visualization. This is called Synesthesia. It's an overlapping of the senses. And the value of doing this is that it makes it hypnotic, and it also allows you to control one by controlling the other. In other words, when you have them turn the feeling of their "Orgasm," for instance, into a colored energy ... when you take that energy and expand it throughout their body, it becomes more intense.

So thats the SYMBOL part ... the color, I most often use as a SYMBOL.

Now comes the **Morphology/Fractionation** part.

Fractionation is bringing someone in and out of trance. Taking two steps forward, one step back, hot/cold, etc.

Fractionation allows you to create a vacuum effect ... where the person gets sucked into the void ... thus closing the space between you ... and intensifying the state, when you bring it in again.

Mind Control Language Patterns

There are many ways to do this, if you're having them visualize. But in my technique, you have to incorporate 3 things; TOUCH, VOICE and VISUALIZATION. When you overlap and combine those three things, you create something very powerful.

So you TOUCH them where they feel the energy... You "MOVE" the energy through their body with your HAND on them ... and all the while, you're guiding their visualization with your voice.

What's more, is it has to be a SHARED visualization. The magic of it is created as you visualize along with them. This creates a SHARED trance effect ... where your INTENT guides the interaction.

This is the reason I think there are so few of us who actually can do this. It's because it has to be a SHARED trance, and your INTENT has to be strong.

So back to Fractionation ... many ways to do this ...

And remember that all of this is just the FOUNDATION for the October Man.

The October Man creates a new hypnotic IDENTITY ... like a PERSON or an alter ego that becomes a REAL entity to the person. This is a new SEXUAL identity ... like a split personality, like having someone over your shoulder who is constantly influencing your every action and thought ... only in a SEXUAL way, saying the things that you suggest. Imagine being able to put yourself into a woman's mind, to influence her every thought ... and to have this PERSONA within her grow and become more real each day.

It's like POSSESSION.

Yeah, that's evil, alright. Which is why we can't ever release it. I have horror stories about it from when we were researching it and developing it. The Synesthesia is enough for most. It's like a nuclear bomb... but The October Man is like a world destroyer.

The Book of Forgetting

by Dantalion Jones

Dedication

To my faithful djinn, familiar and constant companion, Dantalion, the 71st spirit of the Goetia, *"His Office is to teach all Arts and Sciences unto any; and to declare the Secret Counsel of anyone; for he knoweth the Thoughts of all Men and Women, and can change them at his Will. He can cause Love, and show the Similitude of any person, and show the same by a Vision, let them be in what part of the World they Will."*

Mind Control Language Patterns

Introduction

There has now been a long history of me writing about the mind, specifically how to influence and persuade others and yourself, using what I call "Mind Control".

For some "Mind Control" is interesting, for others it's frightening and for a few the topic of mind control initiates a cascade of violent and disturbing emotions. To this latter group, I have sympathy and hope they get a better grip on life.

What I haven't done, until now, is write about a subject that is disturbing to me.

Initially, the topic seems harmless, until it uncovers the real fragility of this part of the mind.

The topic is about forgetting.

Note, I said forgetting, not memory. Forgetting.

There is plenty of literature about memory and memory improvement, called mnemonics, and in studying mnemonics, one discovers that memory can be enhanced. This is a testament to the pliability of the mind.

What few have researched is how to exploit the opposite of memory, forgetting.

The TV show "Heros" introduced a character who can remove memories from peoples' minds, as if pulling grub worms from their heads. From that, I began to ask what would it be like to have this power. Using the skills of Neuro Linguistic Programming (NLP), mind control and hypnosis - how could one make real this power of removing memories?

Does this frighten you?

In learning about and exploiting forgetting, one becomes aware of how fragile memory truly is. This can be disturbing for many, because of the unshakable credence we give to our own perceptions and memories.

Mind Control Language Patterns

On the one hand, forgetting can be a blessing. The hope of many is to forget the terrors and traumas of the past that on-goingly torment their everyday lives.

On the other hand, forgetting even the smallest detail threatens that which makes up one's own personal history.

Forgetting is personal, and when one person forgets something that others remember, it forces the person who forgot to reevaluate their perceptions, or fight fiercely to deny what others remember as true.

This book, The Book of Forgetting, is about learning how to forget and to make others forget. It contains many ponderings and experiments in forgetting, not all of which are complete. The Book of Forgetting has yet to have enough content to be a book in its own right but, nonetheless, is worthy of release. Thus, you are receiving it as an addition to Mind Control Language Patterns.

This is advanced material, but I'll attempt to get as much information as possible in the form of examples, transcripts and analogies. A background in NLP wouldn't hurt you.

Mind Control Language Patterns

The Set Up

The idea of a set up comes from the Neuro Linguistic Programming (NLP) concept of giving process information versus content information.

To make it clear, content information consists of facts that people remember, the price of a product, the date of an anniversary, the name of a lover, their own birthday. All content information is quantifiable and specific.

Process information is more qualitative. Process information is about how we experience that information – as bright, resounding, reverberating, fading, shocking, etc. All of these are the ways we experience the information.

The quality of the process information will enhance or detract from the content information. As an example, let's make the content a hamburger. How we perceive the hamburger can make all the difference and determine if it's memorable or not.

Perceiving the hamburger can determine whether you want to eat it or not. This becomes the process. If you make the image of the hamburger big, bright and in full color and see it rotating on a black background, you will have a much more memorable response than if it were a small black and white image, the size of a postage stamp. As a general rule, your desire to eat that hamburger will also be determined by the process information you use around it.

So let's continue with the set up.

So it's here, in these first pages, you will get the set up for what you'll read about forgetting. This is how you'll learn and how you will respond to what you learn about forgetting.

There is something fascinating about the mind and how it works. Even more fascinating is about the times it doesn't work in the way that one expects. This includes forgetting.

Forgetting includes the feeling of confusion, because forgetting sometimes includes the knowledge that something has been forgotten. You may remember what it's like to have your car keys in-hand one mo-

Mind Control Language Patterns

ment and then not knowing where they went, the next. Then the next moment, you begin to question your ability to think.

Take a moment to remember that feeling and, sometime very soon, you'll remember it again, and curse the fact that you read this, knowing that you may begin to doubt the things you thought about, yourself. But let's not go too fast. All of that will happen in time.

As part of this set up, consider everything that you are not thinking right now.... and you'll find that you are not thinking about a lot. Most of your thinking happens, or doesn't happen, at a level that you're not aware of. This is the level where forgetting take place.

Forgetting also occurs when one thought supersedes another, like when you realize the genius of the writer of this paragraph, and begin to smile, and look forward to learning how well you'll be able to induce forgetting in others.

At other times, forgetting is a mere change of thought. A transition that moves from one thought to the next, seemingly unrelated thought, that leaves the first thought buried deep within the unconscious mind.

NLP often states that, to measure results of a goal or outcome, the stated goal must fulfill three criteria: 1) It must be stated in the positive; 2) it must be quantifiable and; 3) It must be under your control.

This makes constructing a forgetting a bit difficult, because of #1 "stated in the positive," because forgetting is about the removal or absence or change of a memory.

So how does one quantify the removal or change of a memory?

By quantifying the action of removal or change.

Now another conflict arises with #2 "It must be quantifiable" and #3 "It must be under your control". How does one quantify a memory that they can't see, hear, touch or put in a wheelbarrow? How does one control these things?

The question of quantifying a thought/memory can be dealt with by the process that is used to describe it. In NLP, this is the Visual, Auditory and Kinesthetic descriptions that make the memory memorable.

Mind Control Language Patterns

To do this, it's probably a good idea to get as familiar with NLP, hypnosis and other related fields, as you can. The author won't take responsibility for your ignorance.

If you dare, what you will experience and learn are the techniques and theories of forgetting.

... If you remember them.

Mind Control Language Patterns

Starting With Yourself

To master the skill of manipulating memories, so that they become "forgotten," it's important to begin with some personal evaluations about your ability to apply these skills.

The first step is to believe that it can be done and that you can learn to do it.

This is evident, when you review the history of NLP. It was longed believed that people with life-long phobias required a great deal of time to overcome their fears. They were then told to go through many years of counseling to help them overcome their fear. Even after years, there were seldom significant measurable improvements.

On the other hand, the founders of NLP started with their own personal belief that a phobia could be eliminated in one session. Starting with that belief, they went out to prove it - and they did. What resulted is referred to as "The fast phobia cure," plus a new model about how the mind works.

The lesson of this is that your beliefs about what is possible will have a greater impact on the results of your efforts than preexisting theories.

So, when attempting to create a forgetting, first start with the belief that it's possible. It's likely you'll discover new ways of getting your end result that are not revealed within this book.

Another lesson that comes from NLP is that if something doesn't work, GREAT! Learn from it - and do something different. As simplistic as this may sound, it has much more power than you might first believe. For one, it prevents frustration in your attempts, because every attempt will either yield a result you intended or a lesson from which you learn. If you are working with someone attempting to create a forgetting, and it doesn't work, frustration could hinder any further steps, so you would just take note, and go on to something different.

Lastly, broaden your definition of success. You'll learn in the section called "Types of Forgetting" that forgetting takes on numerous forms. Don't get trapped in thinking that a forgetting is successful, only if you have created complete irretrievable amnesia. At times, a forgetting may be a complete success, if you leave the memory of the event, but shrink its significance in the person's mind.

While it may be a goal to create complete amnesia, you'll do better to think of this as an art, where the real goal is to get the best result, with the most minimal effort.

Mind Control Language Patterns

Ecology, Karma and Other Peoples Stories

The origins of NLP are filled with renegades who set out to change people, just to see if they could. This includes people who wanted to find out if they could create a phobia as quickly as they could remove one.

To the moralists and academics, this rampant disregard for peoples' well being created a backlash and redefined the word "ecology." NLP trainings then began to tout how every change must be "ecological" - meaning that every part of the change must benefit the individual.

What many NLPers have done is taken the word "ecology" to mean they must avoid doing anything that is dramatic and powerful and have watered down anything to asking for permissions from their subjects to do every step of the process.

This is sometimes like bringing two lawyers in to negotiate a sexual encounter between two new romantic partners.

The point is that there should be no fear of doing something dramatic, bold and powerful. If something doesn't work, then you can do something different.

The Morality and Necessity of Forgetting

As much as one might cling to the value and morality of "the truth" of what has happened, there is also a value and morality to forgetting.

Israeli sociologist Yehuda Elkana wrote a remarkable essay on the importance of forgetting, as he addressed the Jewish culture that was haunted by the past. He argued that to obsess and fixate on the past and its traumas hindered one's abilities to function in the present, and build the future. Forgetting, he argued was a necessary good. No person or society should be in the grip of the past, no matter how traumatic.

Forgetting has value.

Mind Control Language Patterns

Karma

Karma is that cosmic punk slap that comes from doing something wrong. When it comes to talking about creating forgettings in people, you're likely to get a a lot of B.S. from people that don't like, or even fear you wielding that kind of power.

This is more a result of their personal "story" about what they believe is real.

If you you want power, the only way to get it is to use it.

Karma-schmarma.

Do what you will - and be willing to deal with the consequences.

The Myth of The Eidetic Memory

There is a long-standing concept of the "photographic" memory, also know as an eidetic memory, or perfect recall.

While some people have measurably better memories than others, the reality of a perfect/eidetic/photographic memory is elusive and most often occurs in conjunction with some neurological disorder, such as autism.

On a more practical level, there is the study of mnemonics. Mnemonics is a systematic methodology that draws associations to items that are trying to be memorized. By creating these links and associations, the memory is enhanced.

Mind Control Language Patterns

Types of Forgetting

Because thought is difficult to quantify, so it's true of memories and forgettings. For the purpose of this book, a memory will be defined as a belief that something has happened in the past, from a first person experience. In other words, in order for the person to say they have a memory, they must be referring to an event that they experienced first-hand.

Any change from that definition, for the purpose of this book, will fall under the category of a forgetting.

A sub-category of forgetting is the modification of the memory. For example, a person may have a memory of attending a concert and hearing the band perform a specific song. If they later learn that it was not that band who played the song but a different band, this would fall under this subcategory of forgetting.

Sometimes a modification of a memory can be sufficient enough to render the memory insignificant and functionally "forgotten".

Amnesia of Identity and Amnesia of Specifics.

This is the rarest and most extreme form of forgetting.

Amnesia of Identity is a common plot twist in soap operas, where the affected character loses all memory of who they are and their personal history. When given the chance to see something of their former life, they show no recollection.

For some people, this extreme form of forgetting has a romantic hold over them. This is likely because everything of their current life is unpleasant and discouraging, and by comparison, anything - even complete amnesia - would be a relief.

The fact is that anyone who suffers from this form of forgetting, and is not brain damaged, is filled with an uncomfortable confusion and self doubt.

Mind Control Language Patterns

Because of the thoroughness of this form of forgetting, being able to induce amnesia of identity is very likely to be short lived and fragile to maintain. It, nonetheless, could be done, given a very susceptible hypnosis subject and lots to time to train them.

It should be noted that people who have Dissociative Personality Disorder (DPD) can have a variation of this form of forgetting. For more DPD sufferers, this is a result of early and prolonged childhood trauma that caused them "split" into different personalities. The personalities each have a different function that is kept separate from all the other personalities. They often have lapses in time, where one personality took over doing things they do not recall.

Amnesia for specifics is about creating amnesia about specific events. It's been reported by NLP co-founder, Richard Bandler, in working with one client for stopping smoking, he was able get his client to completely forget that he ever smoked. The amnesia was so thorough for smoking that he would get into arguments with people who told him that he used to smoke. When the subject was shown a picture of himself holding a cigarette, he would hallucinate it not being there, and further arguments would ensue.

This example demonstrates the ecological effects of creating forgettings. One would be wise to consider the overall consequences to the individual when making changes that are this extreme.

[Creating this type of forgetting is covered in the section titled Creating Complete Hypnotic Forgetting For Specifics]

Forgetting of too much information.

This is a very common form of forgetting that deals with the forgetting of information (as opposed to forgetting of events).

Forgetting of too much information is achieved by overwhelming the conscious mind with details - too many details for the ordinary human mind to grasp.

A good example of this is when someone is preparing for a trip and thinking of all the details they need to be ready, only to forget to turn off the coffee pot after leaving for the airport.

Mind Control Language Patterns

Another example is in memorizing long lists of information. Unless there is a lot of practice and some mnemonic devices used, there will very likely be details that will be missed.

Forgetting of the unimportant.

Throughout life, we tend to alter our perspective upon experiences. At one moment in our youth, something can become our whole life - maybe it's our love of sports or our first love for someone. With time and experience, our perspective of these events change.

Sometimes the events become unimportant to us, and we treat them as if they had happened to a different person, at a different time.

Forgetting by means of decay (not thinking about something for a long time).

Attention has a strong impact on memory. By focusing our attention on a memory, we can augment it far beyond the original experience. This is often evident when when a person has a harrowing experience that ends in pleasure. Only the pleasant part of the experience is remembered.

Several years ago, I attended a strange public event in the Nevada desert called Burning Man. The week-long event was, at times, unbearably hot and dusty, and even though Burning Man is a celebration, it was very hard work.

After Burning Man, all I was left with was the wonderful memories, and I concluded that "Having been to Burning Man is always better than being at Burning Man."

In this case, the difficult memories were not focused on and eventually decayed, leaving the remaining pleasant memories.

Another example of forgetting by means of decay is Martina Navratalova. She came to the United States to play tennis from Czechoslovakia and learned English and became a US citizen. After nearly a decade of living in the United States, speaking only English, she then returned to her native country, only to find that she had to relearn the language of her birth. It had decayed from lack of use.

Mind Control Language Patterns

Forgetting by absence of association.

For memories to last, they need to be linked with something. Mnemonics is a memorization system where unrelated items can be remembered in sequence by linking them to things that are already familiar. For example, a person can remember their grocery list by walking through their house, imagining each item placed in different rooms. Thus they would link the room to the item.

Some people have no memory of certain events, simply because, at the time, they have nothing to compare it to. People who have sky dived for the first time often report no clear memory of the first 10 seconds of free fall from the air plane. This is because the experience of free fall is so completely alien to them.

So if you can remove or alter the link to the memory, the memory can be altered.

Forgetting by denial

This one is a process of forgetting that is often employed by bureaucrats whose actions are under scrutiny.

"I have no recollection of that event," is often what is said.

Forgetting by denial has only an outward sign of forgetting. Subjectively, the individual knows more than they are letting on.

Forgetting by confusion

For the ordinary human mind, confusion is a very disturbing state. So disturbing that we will do anything to end it, even if it means accepting something that is false.

Thus any memory that has confusing elements (or to which confusing elements can be added) can much more easily be forgotten.

For the person who wants to play with creating confusion in people, it can be quite fun, but it can also be hazardous. People do not like confusion, and if you make a habit of habitually inducing confusion in people, it's likely they will not enjoy your presence, even if they don't know why.

Mind Control Language Patterns

[This type of forgetting can be created by the processes described in Forgetting by Changing the Process of Remembering]

Forgetting by disassociation (saying, *"I can't believe he did that!"*)

Disassociation simply means not being connected. In the case of forgetting, this can result in an event that is modified, so that the person who experienced it believes it actually happened to someone else.

This can also happen when someone has a memory of the event but simply doesn't feel "connected" to it, as if it happened to someone else.

Forgetting by substitution of memory

Substitution of memory happens when we have a "mistaken" memory that is the result of confusion of details, thus creating a second memory.

Mind Control Language Patterns

Creating Forgettings

There are three main theories regarding forgetting. They are as follows:

Trace Decay

This is based on the idea of producing a trace in the brain tissues. If you could imagine pouring hot water into a bowl of strawberry flavored jelly. The water will produce patterns in the jelly. If the water is too cold, then the pattern or trace will be weak. This is the same for traces in the brain - if the trace is weak, then the information will not be remembered.

Interference

This theory maintains that memory is based on the formation of associations. An item might interfere with the learning process of associating the same item with new associations. For example, when I moved from Croydon to Tadworth, I kept on remembering my old post code, instead of the new one.

Retrieval Failure

The expression 'It's on the tip of my tongue' is used at some point by people who know the answer or the item in question, but cannot retrieve it. This area of memory relates to storage and retrieval. Information is stored in memory, but sometimes fails to be accessed when required.

Cues, like those used in mnemonic systems, make information accessible. If an incorrect retrieval cue is used, then forgetting occurs.

The above three theories hold true for their followers, and as per usual, psychological research indicates that a theory fits best in different situations.

An old hypothesis stated that forgetting in short-term memory (in seconds) is accounted for by trace decay, while longer intervals are due to interference.

Mind Control Language Patterns

These are, of course, theories of forgetting. This book is about *application* - not just theory.

Beliefs That Affect Memory

To start, let's look at how beliefs effect memories. If we believe a memory is not real, then we'll not treat it like a memory. We will tend to rationalize, minimize and justify this now unreal memory.

So what is a belief?

A belief is nothing more than a thought to which is added certain emotions, especially the feeling of certainty. A belief can be augmented by adding other emotional qualities, such as importance, terror or anger.

So what happens when you alter beliefs about memories?

In the book by Robert Dilts "Changing Beliefs With NLP," there are many ways of modifying beliefs by changing the visual, auditory and kinesthetic (VAK) coding of the beliefs.

Using NLP VAK Submodality Modifications to Modify Beliefs About Memory

Here is a transcript of work done with "Jerry," who is plagued with a memory of being left by a girlfriend.

Operator: How are you dealing with the breakup with your girlfriend?

Jerry: It's hard not to think about it. In fact, I don't think I can stop thinking about it.

O: Have you tried?

J: Yes, seriously. It's always on my mind.

O: Would you be willing to try something?

J: Sure.

O: You said that you believe you can't stop thinking about the breakup, so if you were to make a picture of "can't stop thinking about it" - what would it look like?

J: It's a picture of me with my head down, depressed, in a dark background. It's big. Close and right in front of me, at eye level.

Mind Control Language Patterns

O: What happens when you make a few changes to that image? For example, can you take the same image, and brighten it up?

J: Yeah.

O: Now, can you push it away, so that it's not so close, say about fifty feet away?

J: Yeah.

O: Let's do some other stuff to it, like rotate it over your head, so the image is straight up and then behind you, so that it's now upside down and behind you.

J: (laughing slightly) Yeah, okay.

O: And what if you stuck it there, so that no matter where you looked, it was always behind your head - isn't it? Do you think you could get over it then - now - permanently?

In this example, the belief about the memory, "I can't stop thinking about it," was altered by changing how Jerry represented the belief in his mind. The memory was not "forgotten" but modified. Further modifications could be made, so that the memory can become even less important.

It's important to note that, when a subject notices the change like Jerry experienced, they are usually more eager to do more. This is a great window of opportunity to attempt further modifications or forgettings.

This can be done conversationally, as described. It can also be done in a hypnotic state, in which the subject is highly receptive to suggestions.

Forgetting by Changing the Process of Remembering

There tends to be a coding process that we use to access information. When the process is interrupted or changed, then accessing the information is halted, thus creating a forgetting.

This is significantly easier than attacking the thought or memory and trying to remove it.

The following transcript offers an example:

Mind Control Language Patterns

Mary needed some help regarding some worry she had about her job and a possible career move. She was given some NLP processes to rethink her options and then began to pause, looking at the floor and appearing concerned.

Operator: You look concerned.

Mary: I'm just worried that I might not be able to handle a job transition like we talked about.

O: Do this. Look up. Keep your eyes above eye level, and think about it.

M: (Long pause. Her expression appears calmer.) I can't think of it. Seriously, I can't think of it.

O: Keep looking up in that way, and ask yourself, "What incredible things can I learn about myself from this transition?"

M: (Long pause)

O: Ask, "What could be great about this? What would it be like if something wonderful were to happen, as you continue to look about it in this way?"

M: Wow. I can' t seem to get worried about it.

O: Like it wasn't really a concern then, is it?

M: Yeah. This seems like I could really test what I'm capable of.

By simply asking Mary to keep her eyes up, it interrupted the process of remembering the feeling of worry. The question *"What would it be like if something wonderful were to happen as you continue to look about it in this way?"* implied that she will continue to "look" about it (meaning looking up) in this way, and find something wonderful.

Creating Complete Hypnotic Forgetting For Specifics

The pinnacle of creating forgettings is to create a complete absence of any memory of a specific topic or item.

It should be noted that one may occasionally see such a demonstration during a stage hypnosis session, but on a more practical note, this may be a bit challenging.

Mind Control Language Patterns

The demonstration takes place late in the show, when the hypnotist has determined who might be the most responsive of his subjects. He then directly suggests forgetting of a fact, like the person's name. By so doing, the subject remembers unconsciously that trying to remember something that is forgotten is confusing and sticks on the feeling of confusion. The hypnotist may even augment this by pantomiming confusion in asking the subject's name.

This process of direct suggestion for forgetting is likely to work for a very short time. In the process of searching for a lost memory, given enough time, the subject will eventually find it.

The way the hypnotist does this is by suggesting a barrier behind which a thought or memory can be hidden, even from themselves.

The success and duration of this process is effected by many variables. Some of them are the suggestibility of the subject, rehearsal of the process and emotions that are used to augment the process.

Direct suggestions of forgetting are very much "state dependent," meaning that once the subject leaves the stage or the theater, their mental state is no longer the one of the hypnotized subject, and the memory returns.

One way of enhancing this forgetting is through rehearsal of the process and by adding emotions to the process. One such process is to anchor the emotions of confusion and fear. The hypnotist/operator would ask the subject to think of an item or merely name the item (like his name), then fire the anchor of confusion, and then fire the anchor for fear. This "chains" the item to confusion to fear, one after the other. Given a few rehearsals of this process, what results for the subject is first, they think of the item and feel confusion, then they feel terror at their confusion. They will continue to feel terror, until they stop thinking of the item.

This would functionally lock away any memory of the item from the subject.

To test the effectiveness of the suggestion, the operator would ask about the item. Upon noticing the subjects discomfort, he would immediately offer a distraction to keep him away from the memory of the item. This test then becomes a functional rehearsal for the forgetting process.

Mind Control Language Patterns

Doing this a few times will create a very uncomfortable feeling - terror, in fact.

The pinnacle of this type of forgetting is complete amnesia for identity. This is where they completely forget who they are and any aspect of their history.

In reality, is this is extremely rare and happens as a result of a of severe emotional stress or severe brain damage. One might be able to induce this quality of forgetting through hypnosis, but it is likely to be very short lived and would require control of more factors than might be practical.

Example of Hypnotic Amnesia Script

What follows is a script to be used in hypnosis that is designed to induce amnesia, using the methods just described.

Begin to go deep within the mind, so that you can imagine what is truly possible with the mind. For example, a person could imagine that far, far behind you is a place, like a trash can, where you've already tossed away thoughts and ideas that no longer matter. As you place thoughts there, they don't even matter, you don't even have to think about them. Gone from your thoughts. So in your mind, find or create this place... far, far behind you... the thoughts you no longer need. You can start by simply taking a minor annoyance or frustration, and just toss it away... just let it fall away... and feel the relief that follows. You no longer have to think about it. Like dropping a heavy bag of groceries or an overstuffed suit case. Just feel the relief when you let it go... and when you have, just give me a yes response. (wait for reply) That's right. Just erase it from your mind like erasing a white-board, gone from your mind, it doesn't even matter any more, feel the relief. Like erasing a magnetic tape - it no longer even matters.

Now you can do that with anything, and just allow yourself to feel comfort, as you do that.

From this simple beginning, the subject feels a reward - relief - for making something unimportant and functionally forgetting it. The process then can be augmented with further direct suggestions.

Mind Control Language Patterns

Now take a simple thought, your phone number, for example, for now, and lock it away from yourself and your mind. Seal it away, so that all you know is that you can no longer find it. Even if you try, in vain... it's just not there. So as you do that, just notice it's not there, is it? (wait for response) That's right, and you know you're safe to continue with that now and whenever it's suggested, you're comfortable with the process.

This latter suggestion "seals" the thought away, even more firmly. Now the forgetting can be strengthened further, with the addition of emotional responses.

So that when you even try, in vain, to remember, all you notice is your confusion... that feels very uncomfortable... even more uncomfortable... creating an anxiety... even a terror of confusion... until you just let it go... let it just fall away behind you again, even further where you know you're safe... feel the relief, every time you let go of the thought or memory and the terrible trouble, every time you try to remember it ... so now you don't even have to remember it. It's such a bother, so just let it go... gone from the mind, the thoughts. It feels good now to just let it go. Erase it from your mind like wiping away a chalk board or erasing a magnetic tape. Feel the relief now that it's no longer there.

Just as a note on the ethical use of this process, as a general rule, don't do this process to another person, if you wouldn't want it done to you.

Creating Forgetting by Means of Confusion

As mentioned above, in a hypnotic state, a person can create confusion, just by having it suggested to them.

But confusion can be induced by other means that are more covert.

Mind Control Language Patterns

Confusion Technique: Excess Information

The easiest way to degrade a memory using confusion is to add in as much other information to the memory as possible. Some of the additional information can be true and related to the memory, but others can be completely fabricated.

Another variation of this is to break the act down into as many measurable things as possible, to create an emotional overwhelm.

Overwhelm occurs when too many things are demanding one's attention at one time. The mind will often forget when too many details are pointed out. Even a simple task can be broken down into so many tasks that it becomes overwhelming.

When an act becomes overwhelming, it is very likely that something will be left out.

Confusion Technique: Self Reflective Questioning

This technique is done much more often than one might think and has been used to extract false confessions, without coercion, and create false memories. The easiest example of this is the repetitive asking of, *"Are you sure?"* By asking this again and again, it will begin to create doubt.

The next step is to introduce other information, by asking, *"Could it be possible that...?"* Note, they are only asking if it's possible, not if it happened. By asking questions like this repeatedly, the mind will begin to create doubts about what actually occurred. Eventually, the mind can unconsciously make a leap from "possible" to "probable." From there, a less than scrupulous person can persuade the subject to remember having done something they did not do.

As a thought experiment, imagine what would happen if, during hypnosis, a suggestion was made to doubt, judge and question all of one's decisions. Add to that the suggestion of wondering if their strategy for memory was accurate and fallible. The end result would be colloquially called "analysis paralysis." This person would likely be in a terrible mess and unable to make decisions and doubting every thought and memory they had.

Mind Control Language Patterns

Confusion Technique: Pattern Interrupt

A Pattern Interrupt is an NLP term for a method that stops a mental process in midstream. The process of remembering something is a process that can be interrupted in this way. When the same memory is interrupted repeatedly in the same way, then forgetting becomes a habit.

One way of doing a pattern interrupt is to say something that is completely out of context for the situation. So, for example, if in the midst of a conversation you were to say, *"The wall outside my house isn't four feet tall,"* the other person listening understands the words but has no way of putting them into a context of the rest of the conversation. Confusion results.

For example, James is trying to convince his friend Barry that he was talking to a red-head at a party last night. Barry is covertly trying to confuse his friend, and make him think other wise.

James: Did you see me talking to that red-head at the party last night?

Barry: Are you sure? I mean, wasn't it really some place else I saw you talking to someone.

James: No, it was last night at the party. The red-head. Remember?

Barry: Wait. You don't know, do you?

James: Know what? What are you talking about?

Barry: About the red-head, the party, about last night....

James: What??!!

Barry: It didn't happen, friend. None of it. Wait, Do you remember what you just forgot?

James: Huh?

Barry: I really don't doubt that you can't not have a complete forgetting of those events. Jim, (waving hands in front of James face) put it behind you. Done. Gone. (Waving behind James) Good bye.

Mind Control Language Patterns

Barry then very quickly changes the subject to something entirely different.

James: Anyway, that red-head. ...

Barry: The clock I don't have doesn't say it isn't seven thirty.

James: Huh??

The point is that, every time that James tries to return to the subject of the red-head at the party, he is thrown into confusion.

Given enough repetitions, James will automatically feel confusion, whenever trying to think of the party or the red-head.

Forgetting by Disassociation

Disassociation means detachment, and in the case of forgetting, it means feeling as if the memory is disconnected from whatever the real experience was. There is a discrepancy between the visual memory and the feeling of the memory. The subject may feel as if the memory didn't happen to them, even though they remember it as if it did.

An example of this type of disassociation is in the following conversation:

Person A: I can't believe I fucked up like that.

Person B: (shocked and offended at hearing the "f" word) *What did you say?*

Person A: (realizing what he did that was offensive, acts shocked, steps aside and points to the area where he was standing) *I can't believe he said that!*

Because Person A referred to himself and his action in the third person, he disconnected himself from the event.

When you do this, the interesting thing is how people respond, when you say, *"I can't believe he said that!"* They usually laugh, which

Mind Control Language Patterns

demonstrates that they are now disconnecting you from your action of saying the "F" word.

At that point, make no reference to the incident again.

Covert Forgetting by Disassociation

The first step is to ask the subject to remember the incident but to "step out of the memory," and look at it from a distance, as if they were a third person seeing it happen.

The next step is to ask if they could imagine seeing another person there having do it, instead. Then follow with other reinforcing suggestions, *"So you could see X, having done it, and you're watching it. It's not really the same as you thought you had remembered it, wasn't it?"*

References

Understanding Advanced Hypnotic Language Patterns: A Comprehensive Guide by John Burton

Hypnotic Language: Its Structure and Use by John J. Burton and Bobby G. Bodenhamer

NLP at Work, Second Edition: How to Model What Works in Business to Make It Work for You (People Skills for Professionals) by Sue Knight

Covert Persuasion: Psychological Tactics and Tricks to Win the Game by Kevin Hogan and James Speakman

Handbook of Hypnotic Suggestions and Metaphors by D. Corydon Hammond

The Forbidden Keys To Persuasion by Blair Warren

Power Persuasion: Using Hypnotic Influence to Win In Life, Love And Business by David R. Barron and Danek S. Kaus

The Deep Trance Training Manual: Hypnotic Skills by Igor Ledochowski

Hypnotic Secrets of Persuasion - To Sell Anyone! Anything! Anytime! by Cody Horton

User's Manual for the Brain, Vol. II: Mastering Systemic NLP by L. Michael Hall and Bob G. Bodenhamer

Handbook Of Hypnotic Phenomena In Psychotherapy by John H. Edgette and Janet Sasson Edgette

Hypnotize This! by Zalman Segal

Mind Control Language Patterns

The User's Manual for the Brain by Bob G. Bodenhamer and L. Michael Hall

Mind Control 101 - How To Influence the Thoughts and Actions of Others Without Them Knowing or Caring by JK Ellis

Entrancing Relationships: Exploring the Hypnotic Framework of Addictive Relationships by Don J. Feeney

The Sourcebook of Magic by L. Michael Hall, Barbara P. Belnap, and Barbara Belnap

The Gaslight Effect: How to Spot and Survive the Hidden Manipulation Others Use to Control Your Life by Dr. Robin Stern

Gaslighting: How to Drive Your Enemies Crazy by Victor Santoro

Gaslighting, the Double Whammy, Interrogation and Other Methods of Covert Control in Psychotherapy and Analysis by Theodore L. Dorpat

Other Books and Products by Dantalion Jones

Some of these books were originally written under the pen name of JK Ellis and are not to be confused with the writer, Jack Ellis.

Perfected Mind Control:
The Unauthorized Black Book of Hypnotic Mind Control

Mind Control 101:
How To Influence The Thoughts and Minds of Others
Without Them Knowing or Caring

The Forbidden Book of Getting What You Want:
Make The World You Banquet
Starting With a Simmering Broth of Ambition

Cult Control: The Building of A Cult

The Delta Success Programming Audio CD Series

Mind Control Language Patterns

Language Pattern Lessons

The following is a ten lesson course on language patterns, originally made available on the Mind Control Language Patterns web site.

Lesson One: Welcome to the Program!

Mind Control Exercises To Build Success: Is this a novel concept or a practice that's been around for centuries? Honestly, it doesn't really matter. The only thing you need to worry about is whether or not you understand how to use language patterns in mind control.

The purpose of this course is to introduce you to the very basics of mind control, with a view to get you on track to start using the technique to boost your overall success in just about any area you choose.

This introductory course, divided into ten lessons, will make its way to your mailbox. How you use this information is up to you. If you're not ready to change your life, well, it's best that you close this e-mail now to save yourself further anxiety. If you're ready to take charge and achieve - this course and the Mind Control and Language Patterns Book are for you, so enjoy…

Lesson Two will be coming your way soon!!

Lesson Two: Language and Why It's Important to Success

The conventional view of language and meaning: 7% of meaning is communicated in verbal content; 38% of meaning is communicated in vocal cues; 55% of meaning is communicated by facial expressions.

The purpose of this course is to give you a sample, a sneak-peek if you will, at the power of language.

When it comes to language, there is a great deal of opportunity for misunderstanding and misinterpretation. On one level, it's quite astounding that people are able to communicate and appear to understand each other, given the complexity of modern language. On another level, it's true that there's a great deal that can be done with language and the power of language, including language patterns, somewhat akin to witchcraft.

Mind Control Language Patterns

With the right approach to language use, you can actually influence your own progress and the progress of others as a means of determining actions and thoughts. The writer and essayist, Voltaire expressed his confidence in the power of words saying, "Give me 10 minutes to talk away my ugly face, and I will bed the Queen of France!"

To have the same power of persuasion, you need familiarize yourself with language patterns and how they may be applied to generate specific emotional states and related actions.

Language patterns, as the foundation of language, work for many reasons as powerful controlling devices. For one thing, most people make decisions based on their emotional states and responses. This is something that marketers know all too well. Language patterns allow a significant manipulation of emotions and thereby facilitate control to achieve desired outcomes.

If you're goal is to be successful or to drive other people towards success, for example, then all you need to do is learn to apply language patterns appropriately.

The first step is to understand and learn to apply the fundamental language patterns that exist in all instances of language use. You need to develop the right mindset to begin to apply language patterns for either yourself or for others.

You need to fundamentally believe the following:

When you use language patterns:

1. You will create for yourself or anyone else the best and most profound experience.

2. No other person will be able to give the same kind of experience as you do.

3. You will be able to achieve the control you strive for.

4. Anyone impacted by your efforts will give positive feedback.

5. You will be able to provide others with precisely the type of experience they strive for.

Mind Control Language Patterns

6. Regardless of the place, time, or situation, you will be able to apply your knowledge to achieve your goal.

What you'll probably notice about these ideas, these fundamental beliefs, if you know a thing or two about the law of attraction or just affirmative thinking in general, is that this type of approach to any activity is a great way to facilitate success. It's a little simplistic – *but only a little* – to say that, if you believe you can do something, you'll be able to do it. Certainly, if you don't believe in yourself, you haven't got a chance.

Language is important for success, because, with positive language, you definitely put yourself on the path to do whatever it is you set out to achieve.

Let's look now at neuro linguistic programming, the most common method for developing and applying the power of mind control through language and language patterns.

Lesson Three: Neuro-Linguistic Programming (Part I)

NLP or neuro-lingusitic programming is formally defined as an interpersonal communication model, based on subjective language and communication strategies. Here, we're going to consider the elements of NLP, and review some of the ways that this mind control technique can be most effectively used.

We're going to look particularly at voice tones and pace, presuppositions, and verb tenses and their role in neuro-linguistic programming.

Voice Tones and Pace

Before we look at the impact that words have upon programming outcomes, we're going to consider the role that our voices – the tones and pace of our voices – play in communicating messages. The tonality and pace of speech is very important when delivering these language patterns.

Below, you can find the three key tone variations:

Mind Control Language Patterns

The Flat Tone

When you say, "You will lift that bag," without changing your voice – lifting or dropping it – then you are speaking in what is known as a *flat tone* or monotone. What you are saying will come across as a simple statement.

The Rising Tone

When you say the words, "You will lift that bag," and you raise your voice tone, using a higher pitch, you are using a *rising tone*. What you're saying will come across as a question, or otherwise an acknowledgment, of uncertainty.

The Downward Tone

When you say the words, "You will lift that bag," with a *downward tone*, the sentence becomes an order, command or imperative. A good understanding of rising, downward and flat tones will give you a clue as to how modify the impact the words you use.

Lesson Four: Neuro-Linguistic Programming (Part II)

Pace of Speech

Just like the tone of your voice, the pace of your speech has a strong impact on how you communicate meaning. One way of noticing this is to consider the pace of your breathing.

When you're not speaking, you will generally notice that your breath is even. The length of the inhale is generally as long as the exhale. Your breathing becomes modified, however, as you speak. Since you speak when you exhale, the inhales will be faster and shorter than the exhales. When you pace your voice to match the natural rhythm of your breathing, you can impact the attention of the listener.

Speaking as you exhale and at a natural pace, you actually create a number of very small pauses. The pauses are too short for the listener to notice consciously, but unconsciously, the many pauses in speech, however small, help to build anticipation.

As you speak at the pace of your breath, you are creating a subtle cycle of anticipation and relief in the listener, anticipating your next words and feeling relief when they hear it.

Mind Control Language Patterns

"The voice roll" is another type of pacing, often used by evangelical preachers. The pace of the voice roll is slightly faster than speaking at the natural breathing pace. Voice roll is usually delivered at the rate of 45 to 60 beats per minute that maximizes the hypnotic effect.

By varying the tone of your voice and the pace of your speech, you can communicate powerful messages to your listeners' subconscious mind.

Lesson Five: Neuro-Linguistic Programming (Part III)

Presuppositions

To presuppose something simply means that what you want to happen is stated assuming it will happne. It also means that you determine that it is going to happen, and you demonstrate that belief in your words and actions. Linguistically speaking, presuppositions are like assumptions, in the sense that they are assumed, rather than directly stated as fact.

These are the types of words you can use in your speech to presuppose:

automatically, continuously, spontaneously, steadily, instinctively, almost magically, constantly, even without thinking, second nature, unconsciously, involuntarily

Examples:

"Before you automatically open the car door, you should watch the traffic."

This statement presupposes that the car door will open; that you will open it automatically. It also presupposes that there is a reason to hold your nose, once the refrigerator is open.

Mind Control Language Patterns

By using the following words, one can presuppose something is true, factual and proven:

actual, actually, absolute, genuine, self-evident, unimpeachable, real, really, true, truly, obviously, fact, factual, certified, proven, authentic, valid

Lesson Six: Neuro-Linguistic Programming (Part IV)

Verb Tenses of Past, Present, and Future

When it comes to neuro-linguistic programming methods, the use of verb tenses as a means of influencing people's decisions and thoughts is both very effective and very advanced. Once you understand the general principles behind this method of manipulation, however, it is likely that you will be able to use it quite effectively in a variety of contexts.

The general principle of verb tense manipulation is established by the way we use verb tenses, in general. When we speak, we use the verbs we have learned as a means of communicating actions or states relevant to whatever we are thinking or discussing.

One of the most straightforward applications of verb tenses in neuro-linguistic programming involves changing from the present to the past when discussing a problem. The subsequent discussion of solutions and the identification of available resources in the present tense also have therapeutic value, in the sense that they reassure the listener that their problems are in the past and that solutions are immediately at hand.

Changing a statement from the present to the past helps to facilitate movement past the problem and on to the solution:

1. *I am having problems with my boss*
2. *I have had problems with my boss* or *I had problems with my boss*

Mind Control Language Patterns

Saying something like, "You have the option to get a new job, or you can request re-assignment" helps, also, to overcome the feeling that there is no remedy to a problem, or the feeling that the remedy is not immediately available.

Lesson Seven: Methods for Programming the Minds of Others (Part I)

A more comprehensive look at the theories behind neuro-linguistic programming is appropriate. The practice of NLP has, after all, been around for some time, in one form or another. Like most things with a history, there have been many different variations developed as expansions on the basic techniques. This section will take you through a couple of the better known variations.

.

Meta Model

Two researchers, Bandler and Grinder, put forward the idea that people generally use words and phrases in a way that reveals unconscious limitations and faulty thinking. The so-called meta model, in NLP, seeks to overcome the underlying issues and ideas that go into the faulty word and phrase selection.

Metal model questions are designed to uncover the information that is deliberately not being revealed and to challenge the faulty thinking, which often amounts to a very restrictive thinking style, also affecting the spoken language.

The basic objective of this NLP technique is to help people develop new choices, not online in terms of how they think, but also in terms of how they behave. The idea is to get people to stop generalizing and to start articulating precisely what they want, not only from themselves, but also from others.

To use this technique, you have to teach yourself to specify. Instead of saying "everyone must love me," say specifically who 'must' love you - and try to establish a reason! The result is a much more powerful manifestation of your wants.

The central key to understanding Meta States, one must understand the difference between "primary state" and a "meta state".

Mind Control Language Patterns

A **Primary State** is a simple thought or feeling. For example, *"I feel sad"* is the statement of a primary state. To think about a concept like death is a primary state.

A **Meta State** is a thought or feeling about thoughts or feelings. For example, *"I feel guilty about my sadness"* describes a state - guilt - about another state - sadness.

Also, thinking about thoughts of death is also a meta state.

One can take a single state, like sadness for example, and have many meta states about it. For example, a person can feel fear about their guilt about their sadness and thus have three levels of meta states - *fear, guilt* and *sadness.*

As you might see, the above mentioned meta state can be considered a very uncomfortable state and can trap someone into a cycle of sadness, the originating emotional state.

As an alternative, one can start with the same emotion of sadness, and go a different direction with the meta states. They can feel sadness, then relief about their sadness and then joy about their relief. So imagine feeling joy about your relief about your sadness. It's quite a different feeling.

In this way, meta states can be suggested to achieve an end result, starting with any originating primary state.

To "lock in" the new meta state, all one has to do is to ask the subject to notice the originating state.

Lesson Eight: Methods for Programming the Minds of Others (Part II)

The Milton model

A model similar to the meta model is the Milton model, which offers a way of communicating, based on the hypnotic language patterns. There are three primary elements to this model.

Number one, it focuses on building and maintaining strong relationships with people.

Mind Control Language Patterns

Number two, it works on overloading and distracting the conscious mind to force the unconscious mind to work.

Third, it allows for the interpretation in words and by communicating with metaphor.

Here is a sample collection of language patterns used by Dr. Milton Erickson. With each of these examples, a person can make suggestions, without giving a commanding order.

For example, if the command were to:

"Consider why you want to do this," said as a direct command, would create a great deal of resistance, but you could say,

"I'm not entirely sure how well you can consider why you want to do this," thus working the command into a sentence, which does not offer the listener a chance to reject it. This explains why these are often call "weasel phrases."

A friend once NEVER told me to...
After you come to...
After you've...
And the more you (X) the more you (Y)
As you...
...by just noticing.
...in a way that meets your needs.
...what would have to happen to convince your Wondrous Mind to continue this ..."
A whole new way of thinking just opened up...
All that really matters...

Representational systems

One of the things that NLP teaches is that our sensory representation systems organize things in terms of visual, auditory and kinesthetic representations. These various forms the conscious representation of our experience and can be manipulated to achieve specific goals, in terms of how people reflect on experience. If you can insight someone to change the perceptions manifest in their representational system – if you can change your own representational system – you can go on to achieve a whole range of outcomes you might never have thought possible.

Lesson Nine: Speech and Its Power

You don't have to study communication very long to come across the quote that claims only 7 percent of meaning of a message is the verbal content; from their vocal cues, 38 percent; and facial expressions, 55 percent.

The fact is that this quote is largely misleading. After all, even the most expressive face cannot sell you on a point, unless they're actually using language that, well - sells!

Think about the great speakers of history, men like, dare we say it, Adolf Hitler (hey, the man was a tyrant, but he was also one of the most hypnotic speakers of the 20th century). Then there's JFK, some of his speeches remain famous to this day - so famous that even the odd high school kid can tell you it was Kennedy who said, "Ask not what your country can do for you but what you can do for your country." Considering most people can actually quote that famous command, well, I think JFK should definitely get credit as a speaker. Then there are lesser known but no less significant individuals, like the British historian David Starkey, who manages to make hundreds of thousands of dollars as a professional historian, simply because he is such a genuinely fascinating speaker; he speaks ad lib as well as he writes, and that's saying something.

So what is the power of speech? The true power of speech is the ability to transform opinions, govern outcomes, and influence realities. The aim of Mind Control Language Patterns and this sampler course is to show you the little known secrets to maximizing the power of your speech to achieve whatever you want.

Mind Control Language Patterns
Lesson Ten: Using Neurolinguistic Programming
to Create Your Own Success

Language patterns are a unique form of covert hypnotic suggestion. You will hear them often referred to by the terms "conversational hypnosis," "covert hypnosis," "Ericksonian hypnosis" or "covert persuasion or influence" or my favorite - "mind control."

In traditional hypnosis, the hypnotist will give direct suggestions, telling the subject what to do and how to respond. Language patterns differ from traditional hypnotic suggestions in that they are not direct. Instead, the operator often describes a process. In order for the subject who is listening to the pattern to understand the process, they have to go through the process in their mind, doing it to themselves.

The popularity of covert language patterns evolved from NLP practitioners who intended to use it for seduction. They were packaged into "get laid" NLP products and seminars designed for consumption by the horny male masses, too busy to take an NLP course and figure it out for themselves.

For those new to NLP type persuasion, there is this belief that all you have to do is say a few language patterns, and people will bend to your will. Some newbies refer to it with hope that they can "get into someones mind and drive it around."

The truth is that language patterns are entirely interactive.

Your ability to pay attention to how someone is reacting to these language patterns is essential to your effectiveness. When you begin to see the subtle flush of the cheek, for example, it's a sign that something is happening. You may not know immediately what the person is feeling - it could be anger, embarrassment, arousal or simply a hot flash. It could be good or bad. All you know is that something is happening! To ignore it, as most people do, would be a fatal flaw in getting what you want.

Language patterns work for many reasons - one of them is because they bring about an emotional state and then suggest an action to accompany the emotion. Thus someone can be talked into bed, or a business partnership, or sold a product or service - just with words.

Mind Control Language Patterns

With a bit of practice, you can basically achieve whatever you desire by applying NLP techniques and engaging in interactive patterns of speech to guide yourself and others towards your desired outcome. This course is designed to give you an introduction to the whole idea of NLP, as it should really be understood. If you're ready and not too intimidated by the communicated power of speech, you are well advised to now take the next step to develop the necessary skills to manipulate and control through speech.

What is that next step?

Very simple...

Mind Control Language Patterns is a full-length book exploring the theory and practice of NLP as a means of promoting achievement and desired outcomes. Your next step – yes, it's very simple – *pick up the book, and start studying!!*